I0838046

Introduction

Have you ever wondered what truly drives our thoughts, emotions, and decisions? The human brain, with its complex network of billions of neurons, is at the core of everything we experience, feel, and understand. This book takes you on an enlightening journey through the brain's inner workings, exploring its intricate systems, powerful chemicals, and fascinating structures that shape who we are.

Understanding how the brain works is essential for anyone seeking to improve their mental clarity, emotional resilience, and overall well-being. By diving into each chapter, you will discover the brain's unique processes: from how memories are stored, to why we feel motivated, to how sleep restores our mental balance. Each topic is crafted to give you a clearer picture of how the brain orchestrates every aspect of life—from daily choices to long-term growth.

As you uncover the role of hormones and neurotransmitters, or examine the effects of exercise, diet, and stress, you'll gain practical insights into maintaining a healthier, more focused mind. This knowledge empowers you to take charge of your mental health, leverage brain plasticity, and better understand the resilience that shapes your personal and professional life.

By the end, you won't just know how the brain works; you'll appreciate its importance in achieving a balanced, fulfilled, and meaningful life.

Index

The Brain: Structure and Function

The human brain is a vast and intricate network, the center of all our thoughts, emotions, behaviors, and bodily functions. Its complexity is beyond any other organ, comprising billions of neurons, all of which communicate with one another through electrical and chemical signals. This remarkable structure allows us to perform a wide range of activities, from basic survival functions to the highest levels of cognition. To understand the brain's structure and function, it is essential to explore its different regions, the roles they play, and the ways they interact to produce the experiences that make us human.

The brain is divided into three primary regions: the cerebrum, the cerebellum, and the brainstem. Each of these regions is further divided into specialized areas that control specific functions. The cerebrum is the largest part of the brain and is divided into two hemispheres, left and right, each responsible for different cognitive and motor functions. The cerebrum itself is composed of four main lobes: the frontal, parietal, temporal, and occipital lobes. The frontal lobe, located at the front of the brain, is responsible for higher cognitive functions such as decision-making, problem-solving, planning, and controlling behavior. This lobe also plays a role in emotional regulation and personality. The parietal lobe, located behind the frontal lobe, processes sensory information from various parts of the body, such as touch, temperature, and pain, and integrates this information to create a cohesive perception of the world. The temporal lobe, situated on the sides of the brain, is involved in processing auditory information and is crucial for understanding language and forming memories. Finally, the occipital lobe, located at the back of the brain, is primarily responsible for processing visual information.

The cerebellum, located beneath the cerebrum at the back of the head, is much smaller than the cerebrum but plays a critical role in motor control. It is responsible for coordinating voluntary movements such as posture, balance, and coordination. The cerebellum helps us perform precise, smooth, and balanced movements, like walking or catching a ball. Although it does not initiate movement, the cerebellum fine-tunes motor activities and allows for fluidity and accuracy.

The brainstem, located at the base of the brain and connecting it to the spinal cord, controls many basic life-sustaining functions. It regulates essential processes such as heart rate, breathing, and digestion. The brainstem is composed of three parts: the midbrain, pons, and medulla oblongata. The midbrain serves as a relay station, helping to control auditory and visual responses and motor control. The pons plays a role in regulating sleep and arousal, while the medulla oblongata is responsible for involuntary functions like heartbeat and breathing. Together, these three parts of the brainstem ensure that vital bodily processes continue without conscious thought.

The brain's cellular structure is equally impressive, with billions of neurons and glial cells. Neurons are the fundamental units of the brain and nervous system, specialized cells that transmit information to other nerve cells, muscle cells, or gland cells. A neuron consists of a cell body, dendrites, and an axon. The cell body contains the nucleus and other organelles, while dendrites are branch-like structures that receive signals from other neurons. The axon, a long, thin projection, carries electrical impulses away from the cell body to other neurons, muscles, or glands. Neurons communicate with one another at junctions called synapses, where the axon terminal of one neuron meets the dendrite of another. Neurotransmitters, chemical messengers, are released from the axon terminal of one neuron and bind to receptors on the dendrite of the next neuron, allowing the transmission of signals across the synapse.

In addition to neurons, glial cells play a crucial role in supporting and protecting neurons. Glial cells, also known as glia, are non-neuronal cells that maintain homeostasis, form myelin, and provide support and protection for neurons in the brain and peripheral nervous system. There are several types of glial cells, each with distinct functions. Astrocytes, for example, provide structural support and regulate blood flow to neurons, while oligodendrocytes form the myelin sheath, a fatty layer that insulates axons and speeds up electrical transmission. Microglia act as the brain's immune cells, protecting it from infections and injury by removing damaged neurons and pathogens.

The brain operates through a system of complex networks and connections, often referred to as neural circuits. These circuits are groups of interconnected neurons that work together to process specific types of information and carry out tasks. One of the most well-known neural circuits is the reward pathway, which plays a role in motivation, pleasure, and reinforcement learning. This pathway includes structures such as the ventral tegmental area, nucleus accumbens, and prefrontal cortex, and is activated when we experience something rewarding, such as eating a favorite food or achieving a goal. The release of dopamine, a neurotransmitter associated with pleasure and motivation, reinforces behaviors by making them more likely to be repeated.

Another significant network in the brain is the default mode network, a network of interacting brain regions that is active when we are at rest and not focused on the external environment. This network is thought to be involved in self-referential thinking, daydreaming, and planning for the future. It includes areas such as the medial prefrontal cortex, posterior cingulate cortex, and parietal lobes. The default mode network allows us to reflect on our experiences, make sense of our emotions, and form an understanding of our own identity.

The brain also has remarkable adaptability, known as neuroplasticity, which allows it to reorganize and form new neural connections in response to learning, experience, and injury. Neuroplasticity is crucial for recovery from brain injuries and plays a vital role in learning and memory. For example, when we learn a new skill, such as playing an instrument, the brain creates new connections and strengthens existing ones, making it easier to perform that skill over time. This adaptability is also why practicing and repetition are essential for mastering any skill or behavior. Neuroplasticity declines with age, but it is never lost entirely, which means that even in adulthood, the brain can adapt and grow with the right stimulation.

The brain's chemical environment is also essential for its function. Neurotransmitters and hormones influence various mental states and bodily functions. Dopamine, as mentioned, is associated with motivation and pleasure. Serotonin, another neurotransmitter, plays a role in mood regulation, and low levels of serotonin are linked to depression and anxiety. GABA, a neurotransmitter that inhibits neural activity, helps calm the brain and reduce anxiety. Endorphins, which are released during physical activity, reduce pain perception and boost feelings of pleasure. Cortisol, a hormone released in response to stress, prepares the body for action but can harm brain cells and cognitive function if chronically elevated.

One of the most important functions of the brain is memory, which allows us to retain information and experiences. Memory is often divided into several types, including sensory memory, short-term memory, and long-term memory. Sensory memory retains sensory information for a brief period, while short-term memory temporarily holds information that we are consciously aware of. Long-term memory stores information for extended periods and includes different types, such as episodic memory, which involves personal experiences, and procedural memory, which involves skills and habits. The hippocampus, located in the temporal lobe, is crucial for forming new memories and transferring them to long-term storage. Damage to the hippocampus can result in difficulties forming new memories, while existing memories remain largely intact.

Learning is another vital brain function, closely related to memory. When we learn, our brain changes its structure and function to accommodate new information. This process involves strengthening the connections between neurons and creating new pathways. For instance, learning to play a new song on an instrument requires practice and repetition, which strengthens the connections between neurons involved in the activity. Over time, the skill becomes second nature, as the brain optimizes the pathways needed to perform it.

The brain's structure and function are not static; they are constantly changing in response to our experiences and environment. This dynamic nature allows for growth, adaptation, and recovery, even after injury. For instance, in the case of a stroke, where blood flow to a part of the brain is interrupted, resulting in the death of neurons, other parts of the brain can sometimes take over the lost functions. This process, known as functional reorganization, is an example of the brain's remarkable ability to compensate for damage and adapt to new challenges.

In summary, the brain is a marvel of biological engineering, with each part contributing to a complex and finely tuned system that controls every aspect of our lives. From basic functions like breathing and heartbeat to complex behaviors such as decision-making and emotional regulation, the brain's structure and function are essential to who we are and how we experience the world. Understanding the brain's workings not only helps us appreciate this incredible organ but also empowers us to make choices that enhance our mental and physical well-being.

The Magic of Neural Connections

The brain's magic lies in its vast network of neural connections, which are responsible for our thoughts, emotions, memories, and actions. This intricate web of billions of neurons communicates through chemical and electrical signals, allowing us to process information and respond to the world around us. Neural connections shape everything we do and think, from the simplest reflexes to the most complex cognitive processes. Understanding these connections gives us insight into how the brain learns, adapts, and sometimes even heals itself. Exploring the magic of neural connections offers a window into the profound adaptability and resilience of the human mind.

Neurons, the fundamental building blocks of the brain, communicate through a process called synaptic transmission. A neuron is made up of three main parts: the cell body, the dendrites, and the axon. The cell body contains the nucleus and is responsible for maintaining the cell's health. Dendrites are branch-like structures that receive signals from other neurons, while the axon carries signals away from the cell body to other neurons, muscles, or glands. The point where the axon of one neuron meets the dendrite of another is called a synapse, and this is where the magic of communication occurs.

At the synapse, electrical impulses in the neuron trigger the release of chemicals called neurotransmitters. These neurotransmitters cross the synaptic gap and bind to receptors on the receiving neuron, creating a chemical reaction that either excites or inhibits the neuron. If the signal is strong enough, it will trigger an action potential, an electrical impulse that travels down the axon of the receiving neuron and continues the transmission of the signal. This process of communication is incredibly rapid, happening in milliseconds, and it is constantly occurring throughout the brain as neurons send and receive signals.

The strength and efficiency of neural connections are not static; they change over time in response to experiences and learning. This adaptability, known as neuroplasticity, allows the brain to reorganize itself by forming new connections or strengthening existing ones. Neuroplasticity is crucial for learning new skills, recovering from injuries, and adapting to changes in the environment. When we practice a skill, such as playing a musical instrument, neural connections related to that skill become stronger and more efficient, making it easier to perform. This phenomenon, often summarized by the phrase "neurons that fire together, wire together," reflects how repeated activation of certain neural pathways leads to the strengthening of those connections.

Learning and memory are intimately linked to the magic of neural connections. When we learn something new, our brain forms new connections or modifies existing ones. Memories are thought to be stored as patterns of connections between neurons, and recalling a memory involves reactivating the neural pathway associated with that memory. The hippocampus, a region of the brain involved in memory formation, plays a key role in consolidating new memories and transferring them to long-term storage. However, memories are not stored in a single location; rather, they are distributed across networks in the brain. This distribution allows the brain to reconstruct memories from multiple sources, which is why memories can sometimes be inaccurate or influenced by new information.

Emotions also play a role in the formation and recall of memories. Emotional experiences tend to be more memorable because they activate the amygdala, a brain region involved in processing emotions. The amygdala strengthens the neural connections associated with emotional memories, making them easier to recall. This process is beneficial for survival, as it helps us remember experiences that are important for our well-being, such as avoiding dangerous situations or remembering positive interactions with loved ones.

Neural connections are not only essential for cognitive processes but also for physical functions. The motor cortex, a part of the brain responsible for voluntary movements, communicates with the spinal cord and muscles through neural connections. When we decide to move a part of our body, the motor cortex sends signals through neural pathways to the muscles, instructing them to contract. This process happens so quickly that we are often unaware of the complex neural interactions involved in even the simplest movements.

In addition to voluntary movements, neural connections are responsible for involuntary processes that keep us alive, such as breathing, heartbeat, and digestion. These functions are regulated by the autonomic nervous system, which operates without conscious control. The brainstem, a structure at the base of the brain, plays a key role in controlling these vital functions. Through a network of neural connections, the brainstem ensures that our heart beats regularly, our lungs expand and contract, and our digestive system processes food, all without us having to think about it.

Neural connections are also crucial for social interactions and empathy. The brain has specialized cells called mirror neurons, which are activated both when we perform an action and when we observe someone else performing the same action. Mirror neurons allow us to understand and empathize with others by simulating their actions, emotions, and intentions within our own brain. This neural mirroring is thought to play a role in social bonding, learning through imitation, and developing a sense of self. When we see someone smile, for example, our mirror neurons activate the same neural pathways that are involved in smiling, allowing us to experience a similar feeling of happiness.

The brain's reward system, a network of neural connections involving regions like the nucleus accumbens and the prefrontal cortex, plays a key role in motivation, pleasure, and reinforcement learning. When we engage in activities that are rewarding, such as eating or achieving a goal, the brain releases dopamine, a neurotransmitter associated with pleasure and motivation. This release of dopamine strengthens the neural connections associated with the rewarding activity, making us more likely to repeat the behavior in the future. The reward system is essential for learning, as it encourages behaviors that are beneficial for survival and well-being.

However, the brain's reward system can also lead to addictive behaviors. Substances like drugs or alcohol can artificially stimulate the release of dopamine, creating a powerful sense of pleasure. Over time, the brain adapts to the repeated stimulation, and the neural connections involved in the reward pathway become stronger, making it difficult to stop the behavior. Addiction alters the brain's neural connections, creating a cycle of craving and dependence that can be challenging to break. Understanding the neural basis of addiction is crucial for developing effective treatments that can help people recover and rebuild healthy neural connections.

Neuroplasticity also plays a role in recovery from brain injuries. When a part of the brain is damaged, such as in a stroke, other parts of the brain can sometimes compensate for the lost functions. This process, known as functional reorganization, involves forming new neural connections to take over the roles of the damaged area. Rehabilitation therapies that encourage repetitive practice and learning can help stimulate neuroplasticity, allowing patients to regain lost abilities by strengthening alternative pathways.

This adaptability of the brain demonstrates its incredible resilience and capacity for healing.

Neural connections are also influenced by lifestyle factors such as diet, exercise, sleep, and stress. Physical exercise, for example, has been shown to promote the growth of new neurons and strengthen neural connections, particularly in areas related to memory and learning. Aerobic exercise increases blood flow to the brain, providing neurons with more oxygen and nutrients, which supports brain health. Regular exercise has been linked to improved cognitive function, better memory, and a reduced risk of neurodegenerative diseases like Alzheimer's.

Diet also plays a role in the health of neural connections. Nutrients such as omega-3 fatty acids, found in fish, and antioxidants, found in fruits and vegetables, support brain health by protecting neurons from oxidative stress and inflammation. Conversely, a diet high in sugar and unhealthy fats can lead to inflammation, which can damage neural connections and impair cognitive function over time. Maintaining a balanced diet rich in essential nutrients can help preserve the strength and efficiency of neural connections.

Sleep is another crucial factor for neural connections. During sleep, the brain consolidates memories and strengthens the neural connections formed throughout the day. The process of sleep allows the brain to clear out waste products and reset itself, preparing for new learning and experiences. Chronic sleep deprivation can weaken neural connections, impairing memory, attention, and decision-making. Prioritizing quality sleep is essential for maintaining the brain's ability to form and retain strong neural connections.

Stress, on the other hand, can have a negative impact on neural connections, particularly if it is chronic. The hormone cortisol, which is released in response to stress, can interfere with the formation of new neural connections and damage existing ones, especially in areas related to memory and emotional regulation, such as the hippocampus. While short-term stress can be beneficial for focus and motivation, prolonged exposure to stress can weaken neural connections and increase the risk of mental health issues. Developing healthy coping strategies, such as mindfulness and relaxation techniques, can help reduce the impact of stress on the brain.

The magic of neural connections lies in their ability to create and shape our perceptions, thoughts, and behaviors. These connections form the foundation of our individuality, allowing us to learn, adapt, and grow throughout our lives. By understanding the factors that influence neural connections, we can make choices that support brain health and enhance our cognitive and emotional well-being. The brain's adaptability, or neuroplasticity, means that we have the power to strengthen positive connections, rewire harmful patterns, and continue evolving as individuals.

Each thought, memory, and emotion is a result of the dynamic interplay between neurons and the connections that link them. This vast network of neural connections is what enables us to navigate the world, form relationships, and pursue goals. The magic of neural connections is that they are not fixed; they can be shaped by our actions, experiences, and choices. Through the lens of neural connections, we can see the brain as a living, changing organ that responds to our lives in real time, constantly adapting to help us thrive.

Hormones and Neurotransmitters

The brain's ability to control, respond to, and interpret countless physical and emotional states hinges on two powerful chemical systems: hormones and neurotransmitters. These biochemical messengers regulate mood, energy levels, focus, stress responses, and many other vital functions. While hormones are secreted into the bloodstream by glands and travel throughout the body to target various organs, neurotransmitters operate within the brain and nervous system, acting as the primary mode of communication between neurons. Together, they coordinate the intricate dance of bodily and mental processes, enabling us to react to our environment, form memories, and maintain health.

Understanding the roles of hormones and neurotransmitters begins with a closer look at how each functions. Neurotransmitters work primarily within the nervous system and are released at synapses, the small gaps between neurons. These chemicals either excite or inhibit the receiving neuron, triggering a rapid transmission of signals that form the basis of thoughts, feelings, and reactions. In contrast, hormones are produced by the endocrine glands and released into the bloodstream, where they can reach far beyond the brain to influence many different parts of the body. The longer-lasting nature of hormonal signals means they are more involved in regulating sustained states, such as growth, metabolism, and reproductive functions, but they also play a role in mood and behavior.

The distinction between hormones and neurotransmitters is not always clear-cut. Some chemicals, such as dopamine and norepinephrine, act as both, with neurotransmitter-like functions in the brain and hormone-like functions when released by certain glands. This dual role exemplifies the tight interplay between the endocrine and nervous systems, which work in tandem to maintain equilibrium, or homeostasis, within the body. Imbalances in either system can lead to a range of psychological and physical health issues, making the study of these chemical messengers critical for understanding health and disease.

Dopamine, often associated with pleasure and reward, exemplifies how neurotransmitters shape our behavior and motivation. Released in response to enjoyable activities like eating, socializing, or achieving a goal, dopamine reinforces behaviors that lead to pleasure, encouraging us to repeat them. This neurotransmitter is central to the brain's reward pathway, a network of neurons that motivate behavior through positive reinforcement. However, when dopamine levels are dysregulated, it can lead to addictive behaviors or mental health issues. Low dopamine is linked with depression and anhedonia, a condition where people find little pleasure in life, while excessive dopamine activity can contribute to conditions like schizophrenia.

Serotonin is another key neurotransmitter, widely known for its role in mood regulation. Often referred to as the "feel-good" chemical, serotonin helps maintain feelings of well-being and happiness. It influences not only mood but also appetite, sleep, and even social behavior. Serotonin levels can be affected by diet, sunlight exposure, and exercise, among other factors. Low levels of serotonin are commonly linked with depression and anxiety, and many antidepressants work by increasing serotonin availability in the brain. However, serotonin's effects are broad; it also plays roles in regulating pain perception, cognitive function, and even digestion.

While dopamine and serotonin are perhaps the most well-known neurotransmitters, others are equally important in maintaining mental and physical health. GABA (gamma-aminobutyric acid) is the brain's primary inhibitory neurotransmitter, which means it helps calm neuronal activity. GABA's role is to prevent overstimulation by inhibiting the firing of neurons, which reduces anxiety and promotes relaxation. Low GABA levels are associated with anxiety disorders, insomnia, and even epilepsy. Many anti-anxiety medications, such as benzodiazepines, work by enhancing the effect of GABA in the brain, thereby inducing a calming effect.

On the opposite end of the spectrum is glutamate, the brain's main excitatory neurotransmitter. Glutamate is essential for cognitive functions like learning and memory, as it facilitates the strengthening of neural connections. However, too much glutamate can lead to excitotoxicity, where neurons are overstimulated to the point of damage or death. This process is implicated in various neurological disorders, including Alzheimer's disease and Parkinson's disease. The balance between excitatory and inhibitory neurotransmitters like glutamate and GABA is crucial for maintaining mental health and cognitive function.

Norepinephrine, also known as noradrenaline, plays a dual role as a neurotransmitter and hormone, and it is heavily involved in the body's "fight or flight" response. When faced with a stressful situation, norepinephrine levels surge, heightening alertness, focus, and physical readiness. This neurotransmitter prepares the body to react quickly by increasing heart rate, blood flow to muscles, and the release of glucose for energy. However, chronic stress can lead to persistently high levels of norepinephrine, which may contribute to anxiety disorders, hypertension, and other health problems. Norepinephrine also influences mood, and imbalances are associated with mood disorders, particularly depression.

Hormones, while slower-acting than neurotransmitters, play an equally critical role in brain function and emotional well-being. Cortisol, commonly known as the "stress hormone," is produced by the adrenal glands in response to stress and helps the body manage a range of stressors. In short bursts, cortisol is beneficial, helping to increase energy and sharpen focus. However, chronic stress can lead to prolonged cortisol release, which can have negative effects on brain health, such as impairing memory and reducing neuroplasticity. Elevated cortisol levels are also linked to mood disorders, immune system suppression, and metabolic changes.

Another important hormone is oxytocin, often called the "love hormone" due to its role in bonding and social interactions. Oxytocin is released during moments of physical intimacy, such as hugging or childbirth, promoting feelings of trust and attachment. It plays a significant role in forming social bonds and enhancing empathy, and it may even reduce anxiety. Oxytocin's effects are not limited to positive emotions; it also promotes in-group loyalty and can increase jealousy or aggression toward perceived threats. This complex hormone underscores the role that biochemical messengers play in shaping human relationships and social behavior.

Adrenaline, or epinephrine, is another hormone with a powerful impact on the body and mind. Similar to norepinephrine, adrenaline prepares the body for immediate physical action. When released in response to a threat, adrenaline causes a rapid increase in heart rate, dilation of the airways, and an increase in blood flow to major muscle groups, enabling a quick response to danger. Adrenaline is essential for survival, but excessive activation, as seen in chronic stress, can contribute to cardiovascular problems, insomnia, and anxiety. The adrenaline rush, a well-known phenomenon, highlights how closely emotions and physical states are linked through hormonal actions.

Testosterone and estrogen, often discussed in the context of sexual characteristics, also have significant effects on brain function and behavior. Testosterone, although commonly associated with men, is present in both sexes and influences aggression, motivation, and mood. Higher levels of testosterone are linked with assertiveness and dominance behaviors, while low levels can lead to fatigue and mood disturbances. Estrogen, primarily known as a female hormone, also affects mood and cognitive function. Estrogen has a protective effect on the brain, enhancing neuroplasticity and reducing inflammation. Changes in estrogen levels, such as those that occur during menopause, can impact memory and increase the risk of mood disorders like depression.

The hypothalamus and pituitary gland are key players in regulating hormone release, acting as a bridge between the nervous system and the endocrine system. The hypothalamus monitors the body's internal environment and sends signals to the pituitary gland, which then releases hormones that affect various organs. For example, in response to stress, the hypothalamus stimulates the pituitary gland to release adrenocorticotropic hormone (ACTH), which in turn prompts the adrenal glands to produce cortisol. This chain reaction demonstrates how the brain and endocrine system work together to maintain homeostasis, ensuring that the body can respond effectively to internal and external changes.

The balance of hormones and neurotransmitters is essential for mental and physical health. Dysregulation in these systems can lead to a variety of issues, ranging from mood disorders and cognitive impairments to physical health problems like hypertension and immune dysfunction. Understanding how hormones and neurotransmitters interact can help us make informed decisions about lifestyle factors that impact these chemicals, such as diet, exercise, and stress management.

For instance, regular physical activity is known to boost endorphins, neurotransmitters that act as natural pain relievers and mood enhancers. Exercise also increases dopamine and serotonin levels, contributing to improved mood and motivation. Similarly, a balanced diet rich in omega-3 fatty acids, found in fish, and antioxidants, found in fruits and vegetables, supports brain health by protecting neurons from oxidative stress and promoting efficient neurotransmitter function. Conversely, high sugar and unhealthy fat intake can lead to inflammation, negatively affecting neurotransmitter balance and cognitive function.

Sleep is another critical factor in maintaining healthy hormone and neurotransmitter levels. During sleep, the brain consolidates memories and clears out waste products, allowing neurotransmitters to reset and replenish. Chronic sleep deprivation disrupts the balance of hormones like cortisol and insulin, leading to increased stress, impaired cognitive function, and a higher risk of mood disorders. Prioritizing quality sleep can help regulate these chemicals, supporting both mental and physical health.

Mindfulness and stress-reduction techniques, such as meditation and deep breathing, have been shown to positively influence hormone levels, particularly cortisol and adrenaline. By engaging the body's relaxation response, these practices reduce stress hormone levels and increase the production of calming neurotransmitters like GABA. Over time, regular mindfulness practice can enhance emotional regulation and resilience, reducing the risk of stress-related disorders.

In summary, the interplay between hormones and neurotransmitters shapes every aspect of our mental and physical well-being. These chemical messengers are involved in everything from mood and motivation to immune function and metabolism. By understanding how they work and how lifestyle factors affect their balance, we can take proactive steps to support our health

Emotions and the Brain

Emotions play a crucial role in human experience, shaping our thoughts, behaviors, and interactions. Understanding how emotions are generated and processed in the brain is essential to grasping the complexity of human psychology and behavior. Emotions are not merely reactions to stimuli; they are deeply intertwined with our cognitive processes, physiological responses, and social interactions. The brain serves as the command center for emotions, processing information from our environment and translating it into emotional responses that can be both immediate and profound.

The limbic system, often referred to as the emotional brain, is at the core of emotional processing. This complex network of structures includes the amygdala, hippocampus, thalamus, hypothalamus, and parts of the cerebral cortex. Each of these components plays a distinct role in how we experience emotions. The amygdala, for instance, is essential for the detection of emotional significance, particularly in relation to fear. It processes stimuli quickly, allowing us to respond rapidly to potential threats. This rapid response is crucial for survival, as it enables us to react to danger before fully processing the details of the situation.

The hippocampus, in contrast, is involved in the formation and retrieval of memories, particularly those that have emotional significance. When we experience an emotion, the hippocampus helps us contextualize that feeling by associating it with past experiences. This connection between memory and emotion is vital; it informs our reactions based on previous encounters and allows us to learn from our experiences. For example, if a person has previously encountered a snake and felt fear, seeing a snake again will likely trigger a similar emotional response, reinforced by the memories stored in the hippocampus.

The thalamus acts as a relay station for sensory information, directing incoming signals to various parts of the brain for further processing. It plays a crucial role in how we perceive and interpret emotional stimuli. The hypothalamus, on the other hand, regulates physiological responses associated with emotions, such as changes in heart rate, blood pressure, and hormone release. Together, these structures create a network that allows for the integration of emotional experiences with physiological responses and cognitive processes.

One of the most researched aspects of emotions in the brain is the role of neurotransmitters. Chemicals such as serotonin, dopamine, norepinephrine, and endorphins are integral to regulating mood and emotional states. For instance, serotonin is often linked to feelings of well-being and happiness. Low levels of serotonin are associated with mood disorders like depression and anxiety, while increased serotonin activity is often targeted by antidepressant medications. Dopamine, known as the reward neurotransmitter, is crucial for motivation and pleasure. It is released during rewarding experiences, reinforcing behaviors that lead to positive outcomes. This relationship between dopamine and emotional responses underlines the importance of reward in shaping our behavior.

Norepinephrine, another key neurotransmitter, is closely associated with the body's response to stress. It enhances alertness and prepares the body to react to potential threats. Elevated norepinephrine levels can lead to heightened emotions, including anxiety and fear. This is particularly relevant in the context of the "fight or flight" response, where the brain prepares the body to confront or escape danger. In this state, emotional responses are intensified, enabling us to react swiftly to perceived threats.

Endorphins, often referred to as the body's natural painkillers, also play a role in emotional regulation. These neurotransmitters are released during physical activity, laughter, and pleasurable experiences, promoting feelings of happiness and relaxation. The release of endorphins can counteract negative emotions, serving as a natural buffer against stress and anxiety. Understanding how these neurotransmitters influence our emotional states can provide insight into why certain activities, such as exercise or social interaction, are essential for maintaining emotional well-being.

The interplay between emotions and the brain is further complicated by the influence of the environment and social context. Our emotional responses are not solely determined by internal brain processes; they are also shaped by our interactions with others and our cultural background. For example, emotions such as happiness, sadness, anger, and fear can vary significantly across cultures in terms of expression and interpretation. Cultural norms dictate how emotions are expressed and perceived, influencing our emotional experiences. This cultural lens highlights the importance of social context in understanding emotions and their neural underpinnings.

Social interactions are crucial in shaping our emotional experiences. Humans are inherently social beings, and our relationships with others significantly influence our emotional states. Positive social interactions can lead to the release of oxytocin, often referred to as the "bonding hormone," which promotes feelings of trust, empathy, and connection. This hormone is particularly important during childbirth and breastfeeding, fostering bonding between mothers and their infants. In adult relationships, oxytocin is released during physical touch, such as hugging or cuddling, reinforcing social bonds and enhancing emotional well-being.

Conversely, negative social interactions, such as conflict or rejection, can trigger intense emotional responses and activate the brain's threat detection systems. Social pain, akin to physical pain, activates similar brain regions, including the anterior cingulate cortex and insula. This overlap underscores the profound impact that social dynamics have on our emotional experiences. The emotional pain of social rejection can lead to feelings of sadness, anxiety, and even physical symptoms, highlighting the interconnectedness of emotional and social health.

Understanding the neural mechanisms underlying emotions also sheds light on mental health disorders. Conditions such as depression, anxiety, and post-traumatic stress disorder (PTSD) involve dysregulation of the brain's emotional processing systems. In depression, for example, there is often a deficiency in serotonin and norepinephrine, leading to persistent feelings of sadness and hopelessness. The amygdala may become hyperactive, resulting in exaggerated emotional responses and increased sensitivity to negative stimuli.

Anxiety disorders are characterized by an overactive amygdala and disrupted regulation of neurotransmitters. This heightened emotional response to perceived threats can lead to debilitating fear and avoidance behaviors. PTSD, on the other hand, often stems from traumatic experiences that create lasting emotional scars. In individuals with PTSD, the brain's response to trauma can lead to intrusive memories and heightened emotional arousal, making it difficult to process and integrate the traumatic event.

Therapeutic approaches to mental health disorders often focus on addressing these emotional dysregulations. Cognitive-behavioral therapy (CBT), for instance, aims to reframe negative thought patterns and promote healthier emotional responses. By identifying and challenging distorted beliefs, individuals can learn to manage their emotions more effectively. Additionally, mindfulness-based approaches have gained traction in recent years for their ability to enhance emotional regulation. Mindfulness practices encourage individuals to observe their thoughts and emotions without judgment, fostering a greater sense of awareness and acceptance.

Pharmacological interventions, such as antidepressants and anxiolytics, also target neurotransmitter systems to alleviate emotional distress. Selective serotonin reuptake inhibitors (SSRIs), for example, increase serotonin availability in the brain, helping to improve mood and reduce anxiety. Understanding the neurochemical underpinnings of emotions can guide treatment strategies, leading to more effective interventions for those struggling with emotional disorders.

The study of emotions and the brain extends beyond pathology; it also encompasses the exploration of positive emotions and well-being. Research has shown that cultivating positive emotional experiences can enhance overall mental health and resilience. Engaging in activities that promote joy, gratitude, and connection can lead to the release of neurotransmitters associated with happiness, such as dopamine and endorphins. Practices like gratitude journaling, mindfulness meditation, and fostering social connections can all contribute to improved emotional health.

Moreover, emotional intelligence—the ability to recognize, understand, and manage emotions—has gained attention in both personal and professional contexts. High emotional intelligence is associated with better interpersonal relationships, effective communication, and improved mental health. Developing emotional intelligence involves honing skills such as empathy, self-awareness, and emotional regulation. These skills can be cultivated through mindfulness practices and reflective exercises, enhancing one's capacity to navigate the complexities of emotional experiences.

The role of emotions in decision-making is another fascinating aspect of the relationship between emotions and the brain. Emotions significantly influence our choices and judgments, often leading us to make decisions based on how we feel rather than purely rational considerations. The brain's emotional systems interact with cognitive processes, creating a complex web of influences that guide our behavior. For example, the prefrontal cortex, responsible for rational thought and decision-making, works in tandem with the amygdala, which processes emotional responses. This interplay illustrates how emotions can both enhance and complicate decision-making processes.

Research has shown that emotions can serve as valuable sources of information in decision-making. For instance, feelings of fear may signal potential dangers, prompting caution in uncertain situations. Conversely, positive emotions can enhance creativity and openness to new ideas, leading to more innovative solutions. However, overly intense emotions can cloud judgment, leading to impulsive or irrational decisions. Striking a balance between emotional awareness and rational thought is essential for effective decision-making.

As we continue to explore the intricate relationship between emotions and the brain, it becomes clear that understanding this connection is vital for enhancing emotional well-being and mental health. Emotions are not merely fleeting experiences; they are complex processes rooted in our brain's architecture. By recognizing the neural mechanisms underlying emotions, we can better navigate our emotional landscapes, improve our mental health, and foster meaningful connections with others.

Ultimately, the brain's emotional systems are designed to help us navigate the complexities of life, from the simplest interactions to the most profound experiences. Emotions enrich our existence, providing depth and meaning to our relationships and experiences. Understanding how emotions are generated and processed in the brain empowers us to take control of our emotional lives, promoting resilience and well-being. As we delve deeper into the science of emotions, we can uncover the profound impact they have on our overall health and happiness, paving the way for a more emotionally intelligent and fulfilling life.

Mind and Memory

Memory is a fundamental aspect of human cognition, shaping our identities, influencing our behaviors, and enabling us to navigate the world around us. The mind's ability to encode, store, and retrieve information is a remarkable process that involves complex interactions between various brain regions and neural networks. Understanding how memory works is essential not only for cognitive psychology but also for enhancing learning, addressing memory-related disorders, and improving overall mental well-being.

Memory can be categorized into different types, each serving distinct functions and relying on specific brain mechanisms. The two primary categories of memory are short-term memory and long-term memory. Short-term memory, also known as working memory, refers to the capacity to hold and manipulate information temporarily. It allows us to perform tasks such as mental arithmetic, following directions, and engaging in conversations. Working memory has a limited capacity, typically accommodating around seven items, and is crucial for tasks that require active processing and manipulation of information.

In contrast, long-term memory is the ability to store information for extended periods, ranging from days to a lifetime. Long-term memory can be further divided into explicit and implicit memory. Explicit memory, also known as declarative memory, involves conscious recollection of facts and events. It is subdivided into episodic memory, which pertains to personal experiences and specific events, and semantic memory, which encompasses general knowledge and facts about the world. Implicit memory, or non-declarative memory, refers to the unconscious retention of information, such as skills and habits. This type of memory is often demonstrated through actions rather than conscious recall, as seen in activities like riding a bicycle or playing a musical instrument.

The process of memory formation begins with encoding, the initial stage where information is transformed into a format that can be stored in the brain. During encoding, sensory information from our environment is processed through various sensory modalities, including sight, sound, and touch. The brain uses various strategies to enhance encoding, such as elaboration, visualization, and organization. For instance, associating new information with existing knowledge can facilitate deeper encoding, making it easier to retrieve later.

Once information is encoded, it is stored in the brain for future retrieval. The hippocampus, a critical structure within the limbic system, plays a central role in the consolidation of new memories. This process involves stabilizing a memory trace after its initial acquisition, transforming short-term memories into long-term storage. The hippocampus is particularly important for episodic memory, as it helps to bind together the various components of an experience, such as time, place, and context. Studies have shown that damage to the hippocampus can result in anterograde amnesia, the inability to form new explicit memories, highlighting its essential role in memory processing.

The storage of memories is not confined to the hippocampus alone; various regions of the brain contribute to the storage of different types of memories. For example, the neocortex is involved in the long-term storage of semantic memories, while procedural memories, which pertain to skills and habits, are primarily associated with the basal ganglia and cerebellum. This distributed nature of memory storage underscores the complexity of memory systems and the interplay between different brain regions.

Retrieval is the final stage of the memory process, where stored information is accessed and brought to consciousness. Retrieval can occur through various cues, such as context, emotions, or sensory stimuli that were present during the encoding phase. The act of recalling a memory often involves reconstructing the experience based on fragments of information, which can be influenced by current thoughts, feelings, and external cues. This reconstructive nature of memory highlights its malleability and the potential for distortion, as memories can be altered or influenced by subsequent experiences.

One of the most intriguing aspects of memory is its capacity for forgetting. Forgetting serves a vital function, allowing us to filter out irrelevant information and focus on what is most important. Various theories have been proposed to explain forgetting, including decay theory, interference theory, and retrieval failure. Decay theory posits that memories fade over time if they are not reinforced, while interference theory suggests that new information can disrupt the retrieval of older memories. Retrieval failure occurs when a memory is stored but cannot be accessed due to a lack of appropriate cues.

The study of memory has significant implications for education, cognitive enhancement, and mental health. Understanding how memory works can inform effective teaching strategies that optimize learning and retention. For instance, spaced repetition, which involves reviewing material at increasing intervals, has been shown to enhance long-term retention compared to cramming. Additionally, incorporating multisensory learning experiences, such as visual aids and hands-on activities, can facilitate deeper encoding and improve memory outcomes.

In the realm of mental health, memory plays a critical role in various psychological disorders. Conditions such as depression, anxiety, and post-traumatic stress disorder (PTSD) can profoundly impact memory function. For example, individuals with depression may experience difficulties with concentration and memory retrieval, often leading to negative thought patterns and rumination. Similarly, PTSD can result in intrusive memories and flashbacks, as well as avoidance of reminders related to the traumatic event. Understanding the interplay between memory and mental health can inform therapeutic interventions aimed at improving emotional well-being and cognitive functioning.

The concept of neuroplasticity is central to understanding memory and learning. Neuroplasticity refers to the brain's ability to adapt and reorganize itself in response to experiences and environmental changes. This adaptability is crucial for memory formation, as it allows the brain to create new neural connections and strengthen existing ones. Engaging in activities that challenge the brain, such as learning new skills or languages, can enhance neuroplasticity and promote memory improvement. Conversely, a lack of mental stimulation can lead to cognitive decline and memory impairment, emphasizing the importance of lifelong learning and mental engagement.

Research into memory is continually evolving, with advancements in neuroimaging techniques providing insights into the neural correlates of memory processes. Functional magnetic resonance imaging (fMRI) and positron emission tomography (PET) scans allow researchers to observe brain activity during memory tasks, revealing the specific regions involved in encoding, storage, and retrieval. These techniques have enhanced our understanding of the dynamic nature of memory and its neural underpinnings.

In addition to traditional memory research, emerging fields such as cognitive neuroscience and computational modeling are contributing to our understanding of how memory operates within the brain. Cognitive neuroscience examines the relationship between cognitive processes and brain function, shedding light on the neural mechanisms underlying memory. Computational models simulate memory processes, providing insights into how information is represented, stored, and retrieved in the brain. These interdisciplinary approaches are expanding our knowledge of memory and its complexities, paving the way for innovative applications in education, mental health, and cognitive enhancement.

Memory is also influenced by external factors, including stress, sleep, and nutrition. Chronic stress can impair memory function by disrupting the delicate balance of neurotransmitters and hormones in the brain. High levels of cortisol, the stress hormone, can negatively affect the hippocampus and hinder memory consolidation. Conversely, moderate stress can enhance memory formation by increasing arousal and attention. Understanding the nuanced relationship between stress and memory can inform strategies for managing stress to support cognitive health.

Sleep plays a vital role in memory consolidation, as the brain processes and organizes information during different sleep stages. REM (rapid eye movement) sleep is particularly important for consolidating emotional memories, while slow-wave sleep (SWS) is essential for consolidating declarative memories. Sleep deprivation can lead to deficits in memory and cognitive function, underscoring the importance of prioritizing adequate sleep for optimal mental performance.

Nutrition also influences memory and cognitive function. Diets rich in antioxidants, healthy fats, vitamins, and minerals have been associated with improved brain health and memory performance. Omega-3 fatty acids, found in fatty fish, have been shown to support cognitive function and reduce the risk of age-related memory decline. Conversely, excessive consumption of refined sugars and unhealthy fats can negatively impact brain function and memory. Understanding the role of nutrition in cognitive health can encourage individuals to adopt healthier eating habits that support memory and overall well-being.

As we continue to explore the intricacies of the mind and memory, it becomes clear that memory is a multifaceted process involving a dynamic interplay between brain structures, neurotransmitters, and environmental factors. Our ability to remember shapes our identities, informs our decisions, and connects us to our past experiences. By understanding the mechanisms underlying memory, we can develop strategies to enhance learning, improve mental health, and foster resilience in the face of cognitive challenges.

Memory is not merely a repository of facts and experiences; it is a vital component of our existence that enriches our lives. The stories we tell, the lessons we learn, and the relationships we build are all rooted in our memories. By investing in our understanding of memory, we can unlock the potential for personal growth, creativity, and emotional well-being. Whether through education, mindfulness practices, or lifestyle changes, nurturing our memory can lead to a more fulfilling and meaningful life.

Memory is an essential aspect of the human experience, influencing every facet of our lives. From the processes of encoding, storage, and retrieval to the impact of stress, sleep, and nutrition, understanding the complexities of memory is crucial for enhancing cognitive function and emotional well-being. As we delve deeper into the science of memory, we open doors to new possibilities for personal growth, learning, and mental health. By harnessing the power of memory, we can enrich our lives and create a brighter future.

The human mind is an intricate web of processes that allow us to store, retrieve, and utilize information throughout our lives. Memory is not merely a passive repository of facts and events; it is an active and dynamic system that shapes our identities, guides our behaviors, and influences our interactions with the world. The study of memory encompasses various dimensions, including its types, processes, and the factors that affect its function. To truly appreciate the depth of this phenomenon, it is essential to delve into the mechanisms of memory and how they interplay with our cognitive abilities.

Memory can be understood through several models that outline its structure and function. One prominent model is the Atkinson-Shiffrin model, which categorizes memory into three distinct stages: sensory memory, short-term memory, and long-term memory. Sensory memory is the brief retention of sensory information after the original stimulus has ended. It allows us to perceive our environment in a seamless manner, holding images, sounds, and sensations for a fraction of a second before they either fade away or are encoded into short-term memory.

Short-term memory, or working memory, serves as a temporary holding area for information we are actively processing. It has a limited capacity, typically accommodating around seven pieces of information at once, known as Miller's Law. This limitation is evident in everyday tasks such as recalling a phone number or following a list of instructions. Working memory is essential for complex cognitive tasks, including problem-solving, reasoning, and decision-making. It allows us to manipulate information, draw connections, and apply knowledge to new situations.

Long-term memory is the final stage in the memory process and is characterized by its capacity to store vast amounts of information over extended periods, from days to a lifetime. Long-term memory can be further divided into explicit and implicit memory. Explicit memory involves conscious recollection of facts and experiences, while implicit memory consists of skills and habits that are often performed without conscious awareness. The division between these two types of memory highlights the complexity of memory systems and their distinct roles in our lives.

Encoding is the first critical step in the memory process. It refers to the transformation of sensory input into a format that the brain can store. The quality of encoding significantly impacts how well we can later retrieve information. Several strategies can enhance the encoding process, such as elaborative rehearsal, where we link new information to existing knowledge, or through visualization, which involves creating mental images of the information we want to remember. By employing these techniques, we can foster deeper processing and create more robust memory traces.

Once information is encoded, it enters the storage phase, where it is organized and maintained within the brain. The hippocampus plays a vital role in this process, particularly in the consolidation of new memories. Consolidation refers to the stabilization of memory traces after their initial acquisition, which transforms fragile, short-term memories into more durable, long-term ones. This process is crucial for forming new episodic memories, as it allows us to bind together various aspects of an experience, such as its context, time, and emotions.

While the hippocampus is essential for the formation of new explicit memories, different brain regions are responsible for the storage of various types of memories.

The neocortex is involved in the storage of semantic memories, which encompass our general knowledge of the world, while the basal ganglia and cerebellum are primarily responsible for procedural memories. This distributed nature of memory storage highlights the complexity and organization of memory systems within the brain.

Retrieval is the final stage in the memory process and is crucial for accessing stored information. Retrieval can occur through various cues, which may include context, emotions, or sensory stimuli that were present during the encoding phase. When we attempt to recall a memory, we often reconstruct the experience based on fragments of information, which can be influenced by our current thoughts and feelings. This reconstructive nature of memory demonstrates its malleability and raises questions about the reliability of our recollections. Memories can be altered or distorted by subsequent experiences, leading to inaccuracies in our perceptions of the past.

Forgetting is another essential aspect of memory that serves a critical function. It allows us to filter out irrelevant or outdated information, freeing up cognitive resources for more relevant material. Various theories explain the phenomenon of forgetting, including decay theory, which suggests that memories fade over time if they are not reinforced, and interference theory, which posits that new information can disrupt the retrieval of older memories. Additionally, retrieval failure occurs when stored memories cannot be accessed due to a lack of appropriate cues.

The understanding of memory has significant implications for education and cognitive enhancement. For instance, educators can utilize knowledge about memory processes to develop effective teaching strategies that optimize learning and retention. Techniques such as spaced repetition, which involves reviewing material at increasing intervals, have been shown to improve long-term retention compared to massed practice, or cramming. Additionally, incorporating multisensory learning experiences, such as visual aids and hands-on activities, can enhance memory encoding and retrieval.

In the context of mental health, memory plays a crucial role in various psychological disorders. Conditions such as depression, anxiety, and post-traumatic stress disorder (PTSD) can profoundly impact memory function. For instance, individuals with depression may struggle with concentration and memory retrieval, leading to negative thought patterns and feelings of hopelessness. PTSD can result in intrusive memories and flashbacks, as well as avoidance of reminders related to traumatic events. Understanding the interplay between memory and mental health can inform therapeutic interventions aimed at improving emotional well-being and cognitive functioning.

Neuroplasticity, the brain's ability to adapt and reorganize itself in response to experiences and environmental changes, is central to understanding memory and learning. Neuroplasticity allows the brain to create new neural connections and strengthen existing ones, which is crucial for memory formation. Engaging in activities that challenge the brain, such as learning new skills or languages, can enhance neuroplasticity and promote memory improvement. Conversely, a lack of mental stimulation can lead to cognitive decline and memory impairment, emphasizing the importance of lifelong learning and mental engagement.

Research into memory is continually evolving, with advancements in neuroimaging techniques providing insights into the neural correlates of memory processes. Functional magnetic resonance imaging (fMRI) and positron emission tomography (PET) scans allow researchers to observe brain activity during memory tasks, revealing the specific regions involved in encoding, storage, and retrieval. These techniques have enhanced our understanding of the dynamic nature of memory and its neural underpinnings.

Cognitive neuroscience, which examines the relationship between cognitive processes and brain function, plays a vital role in memory research. By investigating how different brain regions contribute to various aspects of memory, researchers can identify the neural mechanisms underlying memory processes. Additionally, computational modeling, which simulates memory processes, provides insights into how information is represented, stored, and retrieved in the brain. These interdisciplinary approaches are expanding our knowledge of memory and its complexities, paving the way for innovative applications in education, mental health, and cognitive enhancement.

Memory is also influenced by external factors such as stress, sleep, and nutrition. Chronic stress can impair memory function by disrupting the delicate balance of neurotransmitters and hormones in the brain. Elevated levels of cortisol, the primary stress hormone, can negatively affect the hippocampus and hinder memory consolidation. However, moderate stress may enhance memory formation by increasing arousal and attention, highlighting the nuanced relationship between stress and memory.

Sleep plays a critical role in memory consolidation. During sleep, the brain processes and organizes information, solidifying memories and integrating them into existing knowledge networks. Different sleep stages are associated with distinct functions in memory consolidation. Rapid eye movement (REM) sleep is particularly important for consolidating emotional memories, while slow-wave sleep (SWS) is essential for the consolidation of declarative memories. Sleep deprivation can lead to deficits in memory and cognitive function, underscoring the importance of prioritizing adequate sleep for optimal mental performance.

Nutrition significantly impacts memory and cognitive function. Diets rich in antioxidants, healthy fats, vitamins, and minerals have been associated with improved brain health and memory performance. Omega-3 fatty acids, found in fatty fish, have been shown to support cognitive function and reduce the risk of age-related memory decline. On the other hand, excessive consumption of refined sugars and unhealthy fats can negatively impact brain function and memory. Understanding the role of nutrition in cognitive health encourages individuals to adopt healthier eating habits that support memory and overall well-being.

Exploring the relationship between memory and technology is another exciting area of research. As technology continues to advance, it has transformed how we store and retrieve information. Digital tools, such as smartphones and computers, allow us to access vast amounts of information at our fingertips, changing the way we engage with knowledge. While technology can enhance learning and facilitate information retrieval, it also raises concerns about potential negative effects on memory, such as reliance on external devices for information retention.

Additionally, the role of social media and online communication in shaping memory is a growing area of interest. The way we interact with others online can influence our memory formation and retrieval processes. For example, the constant exposure to information on social media platforms can lead to a phenomenon known as "information overload," which may hinder our ability to retain and recall information effectively. Balancing technology use with mindful practices can help mitigate these effects and promote healthier memory function.

The intricate interplay between memory and our experiences underscores its significance in our lives. Memory influences our perceptions, decisions, and relationships, contributing to our understanding of ourselves and the world around us. Our ability to learn from past experiences, adapt to new situations, and envision future possibilities relies on the functioning of our memory systems.

As we delve deeper into the study of memory, it becomes evident that memory is not a static process but rather a dynamic and evolving system that is constantly shaped by our experiences, environment, and biology. By investing in our understanding of memory, we can unlock the potential for personal growth, creativity, and emotional well-being. Whether through education, mindfulness practices, or lifestyle changes, nurturing our memory can lead to a more fulfilling and meaningful life.

In summary, memory is an essential aspect of human cognition that influences every facet of our lives. From encoding, storage, and retrieval to the

 factors that impact memory function, the complexity of this phenomenon is vast. The interplay between memory and other cognitive processes, as well as external factors such as stress, sleep, and nutrition, highlights the importance of nurturing our cognitive health. As we continue to explore the mysteries of memory, we gain insights that can enhance our understanding of ourselves, our relationships, and our capacity for learning and growth.

Decision Making and the Prefrontal Cortex

The process of decision-making is one of the most complex and fascinating functions of the human brain, involving a myriad of cognitive processes and neural mechanisms. Central to this intricate web of activity is the prefrontal cortex, a region located at the front of the brain that plays a crucial role in executive functions. This area is essential for various aspects of decision-making, including planning, reasoning, problem-solving, and social behavior. To fully understand the significance of the prefrontal cortex in decision-making, we must explore the structure and function of this region, how it interacts with other brain areas, and the factors influencing our choices.

The prefrontal cortex is often regarded as the "executive" center of the brain. It encompasses the anterior portion of the frontal lobes and is involved in high-level cognitive processes that enable us to navigate the complexities of life. This area can be further divided into several subregions, each responsible for different functions. The dorsolateral prefrontal cortex (DLPFC) is associated with executive functions such as working memory, attention, and cognitive flexibility. The ventromedial prefrontal cortex (VMPFC) is linked to emotional regulation and reward processing, while the orbitofrontal cortex (OFC) plays a significant role in decision-making related to social and emotional contexts.

One of the most critical aspects of decision-making is the ability to evaluate options and anticipate the consequences of our choices. The prefrontal cortex integrates information from various sources, including past experiences, current sensory inputs, and emotional states, to facilitate this evaluation process. This integration allows us to weigh the pros and cons of different options, assess potential risks and rewards, and ultimately make informed decisions. The DLPFC, in particular, is heavily involved in this evaluation process, helping to maintain focus on relevant information while filtering out distractions.

Neuroscientific research has revealed that the prefrontal cortex operates in concert with other brain regions to support decision-making. The amygdala, a small almond-shaped structure located deep within the temporal lobes, plays a vital role in processing emotions and fear responses. It communicates with the prefrontal cortex, providing emotional context to our decisions. For instance, when faced with a choice that may involve potential danger, the amygdala can signal the prefrontal cortex to prioritize safety over reward, influencing the final decision. This interplay between emotion and cognition is essential for adaptive decision-making, as it allows us to respond appropriately to complex social and environmental challenges.

Another important area that interacts with the prefrontal cortex during decision-making is the basal ganglia, a group of nuclei located deep within the brain that are primarily involved in movement and habit formation. The basal ganglia receive input from the prefrontal cortex and help to translate our decisions into actions. This connection is particularly significant when it comes to habitual decision-making or learning from reinforcement. The prefrontal cortex evaluates potential rewards and risks, while the basal ganglia execute the learned behavior, establishing a feedback loop that reinforces or modifies our actions based on outcomes.

Decision-making is not merely a cognitive process; it is also influenced by a range of contextual factors, including social dynamics, environmental cues, and individual differences. Social influences can significantly shape our choices, often leading us to conform to group norms or seek approval from others. The prefrontal cortex plays a key role in navigating these social contexts, allowing us to consider the perspectives and opinions of others while still asserting our own preferences. This capacity for social cognition is crucial for forming relationships and functioning effectively within society.

Cognitive biases can also impact our decision-making processes. Cognitive biases are systematic errors in thinking that affect the judgments and decisions we make. For example, confirmation bias leads individuals to favor information that confirms their existing beliefs while disregarding contradictory evidence. The prefrontal cortex is responsible for monitoring our thought processes and evaluating the quality of the information we consider. By recognizing and mitigating cognitive biases, we can improve our decision-making abilities and make choices that are more aligned with reality.

Stress and emotional states can significantly influence decision-making as well. Under conditions of high stress, the brain often shifts its reliance from the prefrontal cortex to more primitive brain structures, such as the amygdala. This shift can lead to impulsive decision-making, as emotional responses may override rational evaluation. Stress management techniques, such as mindfulness and relaxation exercises, can help enhance the functioning of the prefrontal cortex, enabling individuals to make more considered choices even in challenging circumstances.

The development of the prefrontal cortex and its associated decision-making abilities occurs over time, with significant changes taking place during adolescence and early adulthood. Research has shown that the prefrontal cortex matures more slowly than other brain regions, which can contribute to the risk-taking behavior often observed in teenagers. During this developmental stage, the balance between emotional and rational decision-making can be skewed, leading to impulsive choices that may have long-term consequences.

As individuals age, the prefrontal cortex continues to develop and refine its connections, enhancing decision-making capabilities. Older adults often exhibit improved emotional regulation and greater wisdom in their decision-making processes. This growth is thought to be a result of accumulated life experiences and the strengthening of neural connections within the prefrontal cortex. However, age-related decline in cognitive functions can also impact decision-making in older adults, emphasizing the need for strategies that promote cognitive health throughout the lifespan.

Neuroplasticity, the brain's ability to adapt and reorganize itself in response to experiences, is a key factor in enhancing decision-making skills. Engaging in activities that challenge the brain, such as learning new skills, practicing problem-solving, or participating in social interactions, can strengthen neural connections within the prefrontal cortex. This can lead to improved cognitive flexibility and better decision-making over time. Embracing lifelong learning and mental engagement is essential for maintaining cognitive health and optimizing decision-making abilities.

Technological advancements have also influenced decision-making processes in contemporary society. The proliferation of digital information, social media, and online platforms has transformed how we gather and evaluate information. While technology can facilitate access to diverse perspectives and data, it can also contribute to information overload and decision fatigue. The prefrontal cortex must navigate this deluge of information, requiring individuals to develop effective strategies for filtering relevant data and making informed choices.

In addition, the rise of artificial intelligence (AI) and machine learning has implications for decision-making. AI systems can analyze vast amounts of data and identify patterns that may not be readily apparent to human decision-makers. This capability can enhance decision-making in various fields, such as healthcare, finance, and marketing. However, ethical considerations arise when relying on AI to guide human decisions, as biases inherent in algorithms can perpetuate systemic inequalities.

Understanding the neural mechanisms underlying decision-making can have practical applications in various fields, including business, healthcare, and education. For example, businesses can leverage insights from neuroscience to optimize marketing strategies, improve employee training, and enhance customer experiences. In healthcare, decision-making frameworks can be developed to support patients in making informed choices about their treatment options, taking into account individual values and preferences.

Education systems can also benefit from a deeper understanding of decision-making processes. By incorporating lessons on critical thinking, emotional intelligence, and cognitive biases into curricula, educators can equip students with the skills necessary to navigate complex decisions in their personal and professional lives. Fostering an environment that encourages inquiry, creativity, and reflection can enhance students' decision-making abilities and prepare them for the challenges of an ever-changing world.

Research continues to expand our understanding of decision-making and the prefrontal cortex. Studies utilizing neuroimaging techniques, such as functional magnetic resonance imaging (fMRI) and electrophysiology, provide insights into the neural activity associated with decision-making tasks. These techniques allow researchers to explore how different brain regions interact during various stages of decision-making, shedding light on the intricate networks that support this complex process.

Moreover, advancements in genetics and neurobiology are revealing the heritable factors that may influence decision-making tendencies. Genetic variations can affect personality traits, risk aversion, and impulsivity, ultimately shaping how individuals approach decisions. This line of research holds promise for developing targeted interventions that address decision-making challenges in specific populations.

In conclusion, decision-making is a multifaceted process that involves the intricate interplay of cognitive, emotional, and social factors. The prefrontal cortex serves as a central hub for these processes, integrating information from various sources to facilitate informed choices. Understanding the structure and function of the prefrontal cortex, as well as the factors that influence decision-making, can empower individuals to make better choices in their lives. By recognizing cognitive biases, managing stress, and embracing neuroplasticity, we can enhance our decision-making abilities and navigate the complexities of modern life with greater confidence and clarity. Through ongoing research and practical applications, we can continue to unlock the mysteries of decision-making and harness the potential of the human brain.

Sleep and the Brain

Sleep is a fundamental aspect of human health and well-being, playing a vital role in maintaining the intricate functions of the brain. The relationship between sleep and the brain is complex and multifaceted, encompassing a wide range of physiological, psychological, and cognitive processes. Understanding how sleep affects brain function and overall health is crucial, as inadequate sleep has been linked to numerous health issues, including cognitive decline, mood disorders, and chronic diseases.

The brain operates on a circadian rhythm, a natural internal clock that regulates the sleep-wake cycle over a roughly 24-hour period. This rhythm is influenced by external cues, such as light and temperature, and is governed by a small group of neurons in the hypothalamus known as the suprachiasmatic nucleus (SCN). The SCN helps synchronize the body's biological clock with the external environment, facilitating the release of hormones like melatonin, which promotes sleep, and cortisol, which promotes wakefulness.

During sleep, the brain undergoes several distinct stages, each characterized by different patterns of electrical activity. Sleep is broadly classified into two categories: non-rapid eye movement (NREM) sleep and rapid eye movement (REM) sleep. NREM sleep is further divided into three stages: N1, N2, and N3. N1 is the lightest stage of sleep, serving as a transition between wakefulness and sleep. N2 is characterized by a deeper sleep state, during which the body begins to relax, and N3 is known as deep sleep or slow-wave sleep (SWS), where the body undergoes restorative processes.

REM sleep, on the other hand, is a unique stage of sleep marked by rapid eye movements and vivid dreaming. During this phase, the brain exhibits activity patterns similar to those observed during wakefulness. REM sleep is crucial for various cognitive processes, including memory consolidation, emotional regulation, and creativity. The cycling between NREM and REM sleep throughout the night is essential for achieving restorative sleep and overall brain health.

One of the most significant functions of sleep is its role in memory consolidation. Research has shown that sleep enhances the brain's ability to process and store information. During sleep, particularly during the slow-wave sleep phase, the brain reactivates and strengthens the neural connections associated with recent learning experiences. This process helps solidify memories and integrate new information into existing knowledge networks. For example, studies have demonstrated that individuals who get adequate sleep after learning a new skill or information perform better on recall tasks compared to those who are sleep-deprived.

Additionally, REM sleep plays a critical role in emotional memory processing. The brain is particularly active during REM sleep, allowing it to process and integrate emotional experiences. This phase of sleep helps individuals regulate their emotions and make sense of their feelings. Disruptions in REM sleep have been linked to mood disorders such as depression and anxiety, underscoring the importance of this sleep stage in emotional well-being.

Sleep also influences cognitive functions beyond memory, including attention, problem-solving, and decision-making. Research indicates that insufficient sleep impairs cognitive performance, leading to difficulties in concentration, decreased vigilance, and impaired judgment. This cognitive decline can have significant implications for daily functioning, particularly in high-stakes environments such as healthcare, transportation, and education. For example, studies have shown that sleep-deprived individuals are more prone to making errors in judgment and taking risks, which can have serious consequences in critical situations.

Furthermore, sleep plays a vital role in brain health and longevity. During sleep, the brain engages in various restorative processes that support neuronal health and repair. One of the most critical functions of sleep is the clearance of metabolic waste products from the brain. The glymphatic system, a network of vessels that facilitates the removal of toxins, is most active during sleep. This system helps clear beta-amyloid and tau proteins, which are associated with neurodegenerative diseases such as Alzheimer's. Poor sleep quality and chronic sleep deprivation have been linked to an increased risk of cognitive decline and neurodegenerative disorders, highlighting the importance of sleep for maintaining long-term brain health.

Moreover, sleep has a significant impact on the brain's ability to adapt and learn. Neuroplasticity, the brain's ability to reorganize itself and form new connections, is enhanced during sleep. This plasticity allows the brain to adapt to new information, learn new skills, and recover from injuries. Sleep deprivation can hinder neuroplasticity, limiting the brain's ability to adapt and learn effectively.

The relationship between sleep and mental health is another critical aspect of this complex interplay. Sleep disturbances are commonly associated with a range of mental health disorders, including depression, anxiety, and bipolar disorder. Individuals with mental health conditions often experience disrupted sleep patterns, which can exacerbate their symptoms and create a cycle of poor sleep and worsening mental health. Conversely, improving sleep quality has been shown to have positive effects on mental health, highlighting the importance of addressing sleep issues in therapeutic interventions.

Factors influencing sleep quality and duration include lifestyle choices, environmental factors, and biological processes. The modern lifestyle, characterized by increased screen time, sedentary behavior, and irregular schedules, has contributed to a decline in sleep quality for many individuals. Exposure to artificial light, especially blue light emitted by screens, can interfere with the body's natural circadian rhythm, making it more challenging to fall asleep and stay asleep. Creating a sleep-friendly environment, practicing good sleep hygiene, and establishing a consistent sleep schedule can significantly improve sleep quality.

In addition to environmental factors, individual differences also play a role in sleep patterns. Genetics, age, and sex can influence sleep duration and quality. For example, research has identified specific genetic variants associated with sleep duration and circadian preferences. Additionally, sleep needs may change throughout the lifespan, with infants requiring significantly more sleep than adults. Hormonal fluctuations, particularly during puberty and menopause, can also impact sleep patterns, leading to sleep disturbances in some individuals.

The importance of sleep for overall health cannot be overstated. Chronic sleep deprivation has been linked to a range of health issues, including obesity, diabetes, cardiovascular disease, and weakened immune function. Insufficient sleep can disrupt hormonal balance, leading to increased hunger and cravings for unhealthy foods, which can contribute to weight gain. Furthermore, the immune system relies on adequate sleep to function optimally, as sleep is essential for the production of cytokines and other immune factors that help the body fight infections and inflammation.

Sleep disorders, such as insomnia, sleep apnea, and restless leg syndrome, can significantly impact sleep quality and overall health. Insomnia is characterized by difficulty falling or staying asleep, while sleep apnea involves repeated interruptions in breathing during sleep. Both conditions can lead to excessive daytime sleepiness, impaired cognitive function, and increased risk of chronic health issues. Seeking treatment for sleep disorders is crucial for restoring healthy sleep patterns and improving overall well-being.

In recent years, there has been growing recognition of the importance of sleep in various fields, including education, healthcare, and workplace productivity. Educators are increasingly aware of the impact of sleep on student performance and well-being, leading to initiatives aimed at promoting healthy sleep habits among students. Similarly, employers are recognizing the value of well-rested employees and implementing programs to support work-life balance and mental health.

Technological advancements have also influenced our understanding of sleep and its effects on the brain. Wearable devices and sleep tracking apps provide individuals with insights into their sleep patterns, helping them identify areas for improvement. Research utilizing neuroimaging techniques has deepened our understanding of the neural mechanisms underlying sleep and its impact on brain function. This knowledge can inform interventions aimed at promoting better sleep and overall brain health.

The intricate relationship between sleep and the brain is essential for maintaining cognitive function, emotional regulation, and overall health. Sleep plays a critical role in memory consolidation, emotional processing, and neuroplasticity, while also facilitating the brain's restorative processes. Understanding the importance of sleep and prioritizing healthy sleep habits can significantly impact our well-being and quality of life. As research continues to uncover the complexities of sleep and its effects on the brain, it is imperative that we recognize and address the importance of sleep in our daily lives. Embracing a holistic approach to health that prioritizes sleep will ultimately lead to improved cognitive performance, emotional resilience, and overall health.

Sleep is an essential component of human life, influencing a multitude of processes in the brain and body. It is during sleep that the brain performs vital functions that are crucial for cognitive health, emotional stability, and overall physical well-being. Understanding the mechanisms behind sleep and its profound effects on the brain can provide valuable insights into improving our daily lives and enhancing our overall health.

At its core, sleep is governed by two main processes: the circadian rhythm and sleep homeostasis. The circadian rhythm is an internal clock that operates on a roughly 24-hour cycle, regulating sleep-wake patterns, hormone release, and other physiological processes. The suprachiasmatic nucleus (SCN), a small cluster of neurons in the hypothalamus, plays a pivotal role in this regulation. It receives direct input from the retina and responds to changes in light, helping synchronize the body's biological clock with the external environment. This synchronization is crucial for the timing of sleep, as light exposure can inhibit melatonin production, a hormone that promotes sleep.

Sleep homeostasis, on the other hand, refers to the body's need for sleep that accumulates over time. When an individual is awake for extended periods, the pressure to sleep increases, compelling the body to enter sleep to restore balance. This process is influenced by adenosine, a neurotransmitter that builds up in the brain during wakefulness and promotes sleep. As sleep progresses, adenosine levels decrease, allowing the individual to wake up feeling refreshed and alert.

Sleep consists of two main types: non-rapid eye movement (NREM) sleep and rapid eye movement (REM) sleep. NREM sleep is further divided into three stages: N1, N2, and N3. N1 is the lightest stage of sleep, where individuals can be easily awakened. N2 is a deeper stage characterized by sleep spindles and K-complexes, which are thought to play a role in memory consolidation and sensory processing. N3, or slow-wave sleep (SWS), is the deepest stage of NREM sleep, where the body engages in restorative processes, including cellular repair, immune system strengthening, and the release of growth hormone.

REM sleep is distinct from NREM sleep, marked by rapid eye movements, vivid dreams, and heightened brain activity. During this stage, the brain resembles its waking state, exhibiting patterns of electrical activity similar to those observed while awake. REM sleep plays a critical role in emotional regulation, memory consolidation, and creativity. Research indicates that during REM sleep, the brain processes and integrates emotional experiences, which is essential for mental health. The ability to process emotions during this stage of sleep allows individuals to regulate their feelings more effectively, enhancing emotional resilience.

The interplay between NREM and REM sleep is crucial for achieving restorative sleep. Throughout a typical night, individuals cycle between these two sleep types, with each complete cycle lasting approximately 90 minutes. As the night progresses, the duration of REM sleep increases, while deep sleep decreases. This pattern is essential for obtaining the full benefits of sleep, as both NREM and REM stages contribute to different aspects of brain function and overall health.

One of the primary functions of sleep is memory consolidation, the process through which new information is transformed into stable long-term memories. Research has demonstrated that sleep enhances the brain's ability to process and store information, making it essential for learning and cognitive performance. During NREM sleep, particularly in the slow-wave stage, the brain reactivates and strengthens neural connections associated with recently learned information. This process allows the brain to integrate new knowledge into existing memory networks, facilitating recall and enhancing overall learning capacity.

For example, a study conducted by researchers at the University of California, Berkeley, found that participants who took a nap after learning a new task performed significantly better on a recall test than those who remained awake. This finding underscores the importance of sleep in consolidating memories and enhancing cognitive function. Moreover, sleep deprivation can severely impair memory retention and recall, highlighting the critical role that adequate sleep plays in effective learning.

In addition to memory consolidation, sleep is also vital for cognitive functions such as attention, problem-solving, and decision-making. Insufficient sleep can lead to cognitive deficits that impair daily functioning, making it challenging to concentrate, solve problems, and make sound judgments. Research indicates that sleep-deprived individuals exhibit decreased attention spans, impaired decision-making abilities, and diminished problem-solving skills. This cognitive decline can have significant consequences, particularly in high-stakes environments such as healthcare, aviation, and education, where optimal cognitive performance is essential.

Furthermore, the relationship between sleep and mental health is an area of increasing research interest. Sleep disturbances are often associated with a range of mental health disorders, including depression, anxiety, and bipolar disorder. For instance, individuals with insomnia are at a higher risk of developing depression, while those with anxiety disorders often experience disrupted sleep patterns. This bidirectional relationship suggests that poor sleep can exacerbate mental health issues, while mental health problems can also lead to sleep disturbances. Addressing sleep issues in therapeutic interventions can have a profound impact on improving mental health outcomes.

Sleep plays a crucial role in emotional processing and regulation. The brain's limbic system, which is involved in processing emotions, is particularly active during REM sleep. This heightened activity allows individuals to process emotional experiences, integrate them into their memory, and regulate their emotional responses. Research has shown that individuals who experience disruptions in REM sleep may struggle to manage their emotions effectively, leading to increased vulnerability to mood disorders. For example, individuals with depression often experience reduced REM sleep, which can hinder their ability to process emotions and regulate their mood.

In addition to its effects on memory and emotional processing, sleep also influences creativity. Research suggests that sleep can enhance creative problem-solving by allowing the brain to make novel connections between disparate pieces of information. During sleep, the brain reactivates and reorganizes neural pathways, which can facilitate the emergence of creative insights. A study published in the journal *Psychological Science* found that participants who took a nap after learning a series of tasks demonstrated greater creative problem-solving abilities compared to those who remained awake. This finding highlights the importance of sleep in fostering creativity and innovative thinking.

The impact of sleep on physical health is equally significant. During sleep, the body engages in essential restorative processes, including cellular repair, immune system strengthening, and hormonal regulation. Sleep is crucial for the release of various hormones, including growth hormone, which plays a vital role in tissue growth and repair. Additionally, sleep is essential for the production of cytokines, proteins that help regulate immune responses and inflammation. Chronic sleep deprivation can lead to a weakened immune system, making individuals more susceptible to infections and diseases.

Furthermore, inadequate sleep is associated with an increased risk of chronic health conditions, including obesity, diabetes, cardiovascular disease, and hypertension. Sleep deprivation can disrupt the balance of hormones that regulate appetite, leading to increased hunger and cravings for unhealthy foods. This hormonal imbalance can contribute to weight gain and obesity, further exacerbating health issues. Moreover, studies have shown that individuals who consistently get less than seven hours of sleep per night are at a higher risk of developing chronic conditions, underscoring the importance of prioritizing sleep for overall health.

Environmental factors also play a significant role in sleep quality and duration. The modern lifestyle, characterized by increased screen time, irregular sleep schedules, and exposure to artificial light, has contributed to a decline in sleep quality for many individuals. Blue light emitted by screens can interfere with the body's natural circadian rhythm, making it more challenging to fall asleep and stay asleep. Creating a sleep-friendly environment, including reducing screen time before bed, establishing a consistent sleep schedule, and optimizing the sleep environment for comfort and darkness, can significantly improve sleep quality.

Additionally, individual differences, such as genetics, age, and sex, can influence sleep patterns and requirements. Genetic factors play a role in determining sleep duration and quality, with some individuals being naturally predisposed to needing more sleep than others. Age is another critical factor, as sleep needs change throughout the lifespan. Infants and young children require significantly more sleep than adults, while older adults may experience changes in sleep patterns and quality. Hormonal fluctuations, particularly during puberty and menopause, can also impact sleep patterns, leading to sleep disturbances in some individuals.

Addressing sleep disorders is crucial for improving sleep quality and overall health. Common sleep disorders, such as insomnia, sleep apnea, and restless leg syndrome, can significantly impact sleep duration and quality. Insomnia is characterized by difficulty falling or staying asleep, while sleep apnea involves repeated interruptions in breathing during sleep. Both conditions can lead to excessive daytime sleepiness, impaired cognitive function, and increased risk of chronic health issues. Seeking treatment for sleep disorders can restore healthy sleep patterns and improve overall well-being.

The growing recognition of the importance of sleep in various fields, including education, healthcare, and workplace productivity, has led to initiatives aimed at promoting healthy sleep habits. Educators are increasingly aware of the impact of sleep on student performance and well-being, leading to efforts to educate students about the importance of sleep and encourage healthy sleep practices. Similarly, employers are recognizing the value of well-rested employees and implementing programs to support work-life balance and mental health.

Technological advancements have also influenced our understanding of sleep and its effects on the brain. Wearable devices and sleep tracking apps provide individuals with insights into their sleep patterns, helping them identify areas for improvement. Neuroimaging techniques have deepened our understanding of the neural mechanisms underlying sleep and its impact on brain function. This knowledge can inform interventions aimed at promoting better sleep and overall brain health.

As research continues to unveil the complexities of sleep and its effects on the brain, it is imperative that we recognize the importance of prioritizing sleep in our daily lives. The intricate relationship between sleep and cognitive function, emotional regulation, and physical health underscores the need for a holistic approach to well-being that includes adequate sleep. By embracing healthy sleep habits and creating environments conducive to restorative sleep, we can enhance our cognitive performance, emotional resilience, and overall health.

In conclusion, sleep is a vital component of human health, influencing numerous processes in the brain and body. Its role in memory

consolidation, emotional regulation, creativity, and physical health highlights the need for individuals to prioritize sleep as an essential aspect of their well-being. By understanding the mechanisms behind sleep and its effects on the brain, we can take proactive steps to improve our sleep quality and enhance our overall health.

The Brain in Motion

The human brain is an extraordinary organ, responsible not only for our thoughts and feelings but also for our movements. The intricate relationship between the brain and the body enables us to navigate our environment, interact with others, and engage in complex tasks. Understanding how the brain orchestrates movement is essential for grasping its broader functions and implications for health and well-being.

At the core of movement lies the concept of motor control, which refers to the processes that govern the initiation, execution, and regulation of movement. The brain relies on a network of structures and systems to coordinate voluntary and involuntary movements. These include the motor cortex, basal ganglia, cerebellum, and spinal cord. Each of these regions plays a distinct role in the complex choreography of motion, allowing us to perform everything from simple actions, like reaching for a cup, to intricate skills, such as playing a musical instrument.

The motor cortex, located in the frontal lobe of the brain, is essential for planning and executing voluntary movements. This area is organized into specific regions that correspond to different parts of the body, a layout known as the homunculus. The primary motor cortex sends signals to the spinal cord, which then transmits these signals to the muscles, resulting in movement. However, the motor cortex does not operate in isolation; it interacts with other brain regions to ensure smooth and coordinated motion.

The basal ganglia, a group of nuclei located deep within the cerebral hemispheres, play a critical role in regulating movement. They are involved in the initiation and modulation of voluntary movements, as well as the suppression of unwanted actions. Dysfunction within the basal ganglia can lead to movement disorders, such as

Parkinson's disease and Huntington's disease. These conditions underscore the importance of the basal ganglia in maintaining motor control and the delicate balance required for smooth movement.

The cerebellum, located at the back of the brain, is another key player in the orchestration of movement. Often referred to as the "little brain," the cerebellum is responsible for the fine-tuning of motor activity, ensuring precision and coordination. It receives sensory information from the body and the environment and integrates this data to adjust and refine movements. For example, when learning a new skill, such as riding a bicycle, the cerebellum helps smooth out the movements necessary for balance and coordination.

In addition to these core regions, the brain relies on a complex network of pathways to facilitate communication between various areas involved in movement. The corticospinal tract, a major neural pathway that connects the motor cortex to the spinal cord, is crucial for voluntary movement. Signals travel down this pathway, enabling the brain to exert control over the muscles throughout the body. Other pathways, such as the basal ganglia-thalamocortical loop, help regulate movement and ensure that the brain can adapt to changes in the environment or the task at hand.

The brain's ability to learn and adapt is a fundamental aspect of movement. Neuroplasticity, the brain's capacity to reorganize and form new neural connections, plays a crucial role in how we develop motor skills and learn new movements. When we practice a new activity, such as playing an instrument or engaging in a sport, our brain undergoes structural changes that enhance our ability to perform that task. These changes can include the strengthening of synapses, the formation of new connections between neurons, and even the recruitment of additional brain regions to support the new skill.

One fascinating aspect of movement is the role of feedback in motor control. The brain continuously receives sensory input from the body, allowing it to monitor movements in real-time and make adjustments as necessary. For instance, when reaching for an object, sensory receptors in the muscles, joints, and skin provide information about the position and movement of the arm. This sensory feedback is processed by the brain, enabling it to correct any errors and improve the accuracy of the movement.

This process of feedback and adjustment is especially evident in skilled activities that require precision, such as playing sports or performing surgery. Athletes, for example, rely on their brain's ability to integrate sensory information and adjust their movements accordingly. This ability to adapt in response to changing conditions is essential for success in dynamic environments, where split-second decisions can make all the difference.

The concept of motor learning is closely related to the brain's ability to adapt and refine movement patterns. Motor learning involves acquiring new skills through practice and experience, leading to long-term changes in the brain's structure and function. Research has shown that repeated practice of a movement leads to improved performance and efficiency. This is often seen in athletes who refine their techniques over time, allowing them to perform with greater precision and control.

One interesting phenomenon associated with motor learning is the idea of "muscle memory." While this term is commonly used, it is important to note that it refers to changes in the brain rather than the muscles themselves. When we repeatedly perform a movement, the brain becomes more efficient at activating the necessary motor pathways. This means that over time, the execution of the movement requires less conscious effort, allowing for smoother and more fluid motion. Muscle memory plays a significant role in activities ranging from playing a musical instrument to typing on a keyboard, illustrating the brain's remarkable ability to streamline movement.

The brain's involvement in movement is not limited to physical actions; it also encompasses our emotional and cognitive states. The way we move can be influenced by our feelings, thoughts, and motivations. For instance, when we are excited or motivated, our movements may become more energetic and fluid. Conversely, feelings of fatigue or sadness can lead to sluggish or hesitant motions. This connection between emotion and movement highlights the brain's role in integrating different aspects of our experience.

Furthermore, the brain's perception of movement can be affected by our surroundings and experiences. Mirror neurons, a type of neuron that activates both when we perform an action and when we observe someone else performing the same action, play a key role in this phenomenon. These neurons are thought to contribute to our ability to understand and empathize with others, as they allow us to mentally simulate actions we observe. This understanding of movement in others can influence our own movements, whether in social interactions or coordinated activities like dance.

The relationship between movement and brain health is a critical area of research. Engaging in physical activity has been shown to have numerous benefits for brain function and overall well-being. Regular exercise promotes the release of neurotrophic factors, which support the growth and survival of neurons. Physical activity also enhances blood flow to the brain, providing essential nutrients and oxygen while promoting the clearance of waste products. These processes contribute to improved cognitive function, emotional well-being, and reduced risk of neurodegenerative diseases.

Incorporating movement into our daily lives is essential for maintaining brain health. Activities such as walking, dancing, swimming, or practicing yoga not only provide physical benefits but also stimulate cognitive function. Exercise has been linked to improved memory, attention, and executive function, making it a powerful tool for enhancing brain performance. Additionally, engaging in social activities that involve movement, such as team sports or group classes, can foster connections with others, further supporting emotional well-being.

The impact of movement on brain health is particularly relevant in the context of aging. As we age, the brain undergoes various changes that can affect cognitive function. Engaging in regular physical activity has been shown to mitigate some of these effects, promoting neuroplasticity and reducing the risk of cognitive decline. Older adults who remain active often experience better cognitive performance, enhanced memory, and improved overall health compared to their sedentary peers.

In recent years, the concept of embodied cognition has gained traction in the field of neuroscience. This theory posits that our cognitive processes are deeply intertwined with our bodily experiences. In other words, the way we move and interact with our environment influences our thoughts and emotions. This perspective underscores the importance of movement in shaping our cognitive experiences, highlighting the interconnectedness of mind and body.

For instance, studies have shown that adopting specific postures can influence our mental states. Standing tall with an open posture can enhance feelings of confidence and positivity, while slouching may contribute to feelings of sadness or defeat. This relationship between body language and mental state emphasizes the role of movement in shaping our emotional and cognitive experiences.

Moreover, movement-based interventions, such as dance therapy or mindfulness practices that incorporate movement, have been shown to promote emotional regulation and cognitive flexibility. These approaches recognize the potential of movement to enhance mental health and well-being, offering alternative avenues for addressing emotional challenges.

As technology continues to evolve, innovative approaches to movement and brain health are emerging. Virtual reality (VR) and interactive gaming are being explored as tools for enhancing motor skills and cognitive function. These technologies provide immersive environments that engage the brain in novel ways, allowing individuals to practice movement and coordination in a controlled setting. Research indicates that VR-based training can lead to improvements in motor performance and cognitive abilities, making it a promising area for future exploration.

The exploration of the brain in motion is a multidisciplinary endeavor, bringing together insights from neuroscience, psychology, kinesiology, and rehabilitation sciences. Understanding the intricate relationship between the brain and movement has profound implications for various fields, including education, healthcare, and sports performance. Educators can leverage this knowledge to develop curricula that integrate movement into learning, fostering engagement and cognitive development.

In healthcare, rehabilitation programs that emphasize movement can support individuals recovering from injuries or surgeries. By focusing on the connection between movement and brain function, clinicians can design interventions that promote optimal recovery and enhance overall well-being. Similarly, coaches and trainers can apply principles of motor learning to enhance athletic performance, optimizing training regimens to improve movement efficiency and skill acquisition.

In conclusion, the brain in motion is a complex and fascinating topic that underscores the interconnectedness of movement, cognition, and emotion. Understanding how the brain orchestrates movement provides valuable insights into improving motor skills, enhancing cognitive function, and promoting overall health and well-being. As we continue to explore this intricate relationship, we can harness the power of movement to unlock the full potential of the human brain, paving the way for a healthier and more active future.

Stress and Resilience

Stress is an inevitable part of human life, affecting individuals across various ages, cultures, and backgrounds. It is the body's response to challenges or demands, triggering a series of physiological and psychological changes. While stress can sometimes be beneficial, enhancing performance and motivating individuals to tackle challenges, chronic stress can lead to significant health issues, impacting both mental and physical well-being. Understanding stress and developing resilience is crucial for navigating life's challenges effectively.

At its core, stress is a complex interplay between the mind and body. When faced with a stressor, the brain activates the hypothalamic-pituitary-adrenal (HPA) axis, leading to the release of hormones such as cortisol and adrenaline. These hormones prepare the body for a "fight or flight" response, enabling quick reactions to perceived threats. This physiological response is essential for survival, allowing humans to respond to danger effectively. However, when stress becomes chronic, it can lead to negative health outcomes, including anxiety, depression, heart disease, and weakened immune function.

Chronic stress arises from ongoing pressures, such as work-related challenges, financial difficulties, or interpersonal conflicts. Unlike acute stress, which is short-lived and often resolved once the threat is removed, chronic stress persists over time and can lead to long-term health problems. Individuals who experience chronic stress may find themselves in a continuous state of heightened alertness, leading to fatigue, irritability, and difficulty concentrating.

Recognizing the signs of stress is essential for addressing it effectively. Common symptoms include physical manifestations such as headaches, muscle tension, and gastrointestinal issues, as well as psychological symptoms like anxiety, mood swings, and difficulty sleeping. Individuals may also experience behavioral changes, such as increased substance use, withdrawal from social activities, or changes in appetite. By identifying these symptoms, individuals can take proactive steps to manage their stress levels and promote resilience.

Resilience is the ability to adapt to stressors and bounce back from adversity. It is not a fixed trait but rather a dynamic process that can be developed over time. Resilient individuals are better equipped to cope with challenges, maintain a positive outlook, and recover from setbacks. They possess a range of skills and strategies that enable them to navigate stress effectively, making resilience a vital component of mental health.

One key factor in developing resilience is a strong support network. Social connections play a critical role in buffering the effects of stress. Friends, family, and colleagues can provide emotional support, practical assistance, and a sense of belonging. When individuals face stressors, having someone to talk to can help them process their feelings and gain perspective on the situation. Building and maintaining healthy relationships fosters resilience and enhances an individual's ability to cope with stress.

Another essential aspect of resilience is the development of coping strategies. Effective coping mechanisms can be classified into two main categories: problem-focused and emotion-focused coping. Problem-focused coping involves actively addressing the stressor to reduce its impact, while emotion-focused coping aims to manage the emotional response to stress. Both strategies can be beneficial, depending on the situation. For example, if a person is facing a tight deadline at work, problem-focused coping may involve organizing tasks and prioritizing responsibilities, while emotion-focused coping may include practices like mindfulness or deep breathing to manage anxiety.

Practicing mindfulness is an effective technique for managing stress and enhancing resilience. Mindfulness involves paying attention to the present moment without judgment. This practice helps individuals develop greater awareness of their thoughts and feelings, allowing them to respond to stressors with greater clarity and calmness. Research has shown that mindfulness-based interventions can reduce symptoms of anxiety and depression while enhancing overall well-being. Techniques such as meditation, yoga, and mindful breathing can be incorporated into daily routines to cultivate mindfulness and promote resilience.

Physical activity is another powerful tool for managing stress. Regular exercise releases endorphins, the body's natural mood lifters, and helps reduce tension. Engaging in physical activity not only improves physical health but also enhances mental well-being. Exercise provides an opportunity to clear the mind, release pent-up energy, and improve sleep quality. Whether through walking, running, dancing, or participating in sports, finding an enjoyable form of exercise can be a vital component of a resilience-building strategy.

Developing a positive mindset is also crucial for fostering resilience. Individuals with a positive outlook tend to view challenges as opportunities for growth rather than insurmountable obstacles. This shift in perspective can enhance problem-solving abilities and increase motivation to tackle difficult situations. Cultivating gratitude, practicing self-compassion, and focusing on personal strengths can contribute to a more positive mindset. Techniques such as journaling, where individuals reflect on positive experiences and accomplishments, can help reinforce this mindset.

Another essential element of resilience is self-efficacy, the belief in one's ability to overcome challenges. Individuals with high self-efficacy are more likely to persist in the face of adversity and approach challenges with confidence. Building self-efficacy involves setting achievable goals and celebrating progress along the way. By recognizing their capabilities and successes, individuals can strengthen their belief in their ability to cope with stress and adversity.

Emotional regulation is a critical skill for managing stress effectively. Being able to recognize, understand, and manage one's emotions is vital for navigating difficult situations. Emotion regulation strategies can include reframing negative thoughts, practicing relaxation techniques, or engaging in creative outlets. By developing emotional awareness and regulation skills, individuals can reduce the impact of stress on their mental health and overall well-being.

In the workplace, promoting resilience can lead to a healthier and more productive environment. Organizations that prioritize employee well-being and offer resources for stress management create a culture of resilience. This can include providing access to mental health services, offering flexible work arrangements, and promoting a healthy work-life balance. Encouraging open communication and fostering a supportive workplace culture can help employees feel valued and empowered to cope with stress effectively.

Education systems can also play a role in building resilience in students. Teaching skills such as emotional regulation, problem-solving, and mindfulness can equip young people with the tools they need to navigate challenges effectively. Schools that incorporate social-emotional learning into their curricula create an environment where students can develop resilience and cope with stressors more effectively.

Despite the many challenges associated with stress, it is important to recognize that it can also serve as a catalyst for growth and positive change. Many individuals emerge from stressful experiences with newfound strength, clarity, and perspective. This phenomenon, often referred to as post-traumatic growth, highlights the potential for resilience to develop through adversity. Individuals who experience significant stress may find that they have a greater appreciation for life, improved relationships, and a deeper sense of purpose.

Building resilience is a lifelong journey that requires ongoing effort and commitment. As individuals encounter new challenges throughout their lives, the strategies and skills they develop can help them navigate these experiences more effectively. Embracing the ups and downs of life with a resilient mindset allows individuals to bounce back from setbacks and approach future challenges with confidence.

It is essential to recognize that everyone's experience with stress is unique. What works for one individual may not be effective for another. Therefore, it is crucial for individuals to explore different coping strategies and resilience-building techniques to discover what resonates with them. This individualized approach empowers individuals to take charge of their mental health and well-being.

Ultimately, the relationship between stress and resilience is complex and multifaceted. Stress is a natural part of life, and while it can pose significant challenges, it also presents opportunities for growth and development. By cultivating resilience, individuals can enhance their ability to cope with stressors, navigate adversity, and emerge stronger from difficult experiences. Understanding the interplay between stress and resilience is essential for fostering mental health and well-being in an increasingly complex world.

In conclusion, stress is an integral part of the human experience, affecting everyone in various ways. While it can lead to negative health outcomes when experienced chronically, developing resilience is crucial for coping with stress effectively. Building a strong support network, developing coping strategies, practicing mindfulness, engaging in physical activity, and cultivating a positive mindset are all essential components of resilience. As individuals navigate life's challenges, the skills and strategies they develop can empower them to face adversity with confidence, ultimately promoting mental health and well-being. Embracing stress as a natural part of life and focusing on resilience can lead to personal growth, improved relationships, and a deeper sense of purpose.

Mental Health and Neuroscience

Mental health is a critical component of overall well-being, encompassing emotional, psychological, and social aspects that affect how individuals think, feel, and behave. The interplay between mental health and neuroscience has gained considerable attention in recent years, as advances in our understanding of the brain have profound implications for diagnosing, treating, and preventing mental health disorders. Neuroscience, the scientific study of the nervous system, provides valuable insights into how brain structure, function, and chemistry influence mental health, shedding light on the biological underpinnings of various psychological conditions.

At the core of mental health issues lies the brain, a complex organ responsible for processing thoughts, emotions, and behaviors. Neurotransmitters, the chemical messengers that facilitate communication between neurons, play a vital role in regulating mood, cognition, and behavior. Imbalances in neurotransmitter systems have been implicated in several mental health disorders, including depression, anxiety, schizophrenia, and bipolar disorder. For example, serotonin, often referred to as the "feel-good" neurotransmitter, is critical for mood regulation. Low levels of serotonin are associated with depressive symptoms, leading to the development of selective serotonin reuptake inhibitors (SSRIs) as a common treatment option for depression.

In addition to neurotransmitters, brain structure and connectivity are crucial factors in mental health. Neuroimaging techniques, such as magnetic resonance imaging (MRI) and functional MRI (fMRI), have allowed researchers to observe changes in brain structure and function associated with various mental health conditions. For instance, studies have shown that individuals with major depressive disorder often exhibit alterations in brain regions associated with emotion regulation, such as the prefrontal cortex and the amygdala. These findings highlight the importance of understanding the biological basis of mental health disorders and the potential for targeted interventions based on these insights.

Stress is another significant factor influencing mental health and is intricately connected to neuroscience. The body's stress response is regulated by the hypothalamic-pituitary-adrenal (HPA) axis, which controls the release of cortisol, a hormone that prepares the body to respond to threats. Chronic stress can lead to dysregulation of the HPA axis, resulting in prolonged elevation of cortisol levels, which can negatively impact brain function and mental health. Research has shown that chronic stress is linked to structural changes in the brain, including atrophy of the hippocampus, a region critical for memory and learning. Understanding the relationship between stress and mental health is essential for developing effective interventions to mitigate the adverse effects of stress on psychological well-being.

Psychological disorders often have a complex interplay of genetic, environmental, and neurobiological factors. Genetic predispositions can influence an individual's susceptibility to mental health conditions, with twin and family studies indicating that many disorders have a heritable component. However, environmental factors, such as trauma, socioeconomic status, and social support, also play a crucial role in shaping mental health outcomes. For example, adverse childhood experiences, including abuse or neglect, can lead to lasting changes in brain development and increase the risk of developing mental health disorders later in life. Understanding these interactions is vital for a holistic approach to mental health treatment and prevention.

The field of neuroscience has also advanced our understanding of the mechanisms underlying treatment approaches for mental health disorders. Psychopharmacology, the study of how drugs affect mood and behavior, has led to the development of various medications targeting specific neurotransmitter systems. In addition to traditional pharmacological treatments, psychotherapy has been shown to induce neurobiological changes that contribute to therapeutic outcomes. For instance, cognitive-behavioral therapy (CBT) has been associated with increased connectivity in brain networks involved in emotion regulation and cognitive control. These findings suggest that psychological interventions can result in lasting changes in brain function, highlighting the potential for integrated treatment approaches that combine pharmacological and psychotherapeutic strategies.

Emerging research in neuroscience has also focused on the role of neuroplasticity in mental health. Neuroplasticity refers to the brain's ability to reorganize itself by forming new neural connections throughout life. This adaptability is crucial for recovery from mental health disorders, as it enables individuals to develop new coping strategies and improve emotional regulation. For instance, mindfulness-based interventions have been shown to enhance neuroplasticity and promote resilience in individuals with anxiety and depression. By fostering neuroplasticity, individuals can strengthen positive neural pathways and improve their overall mental health.

Another exciting area of research within the field of neuroscience and mental health is the exploration of the gut-brain connection. The gut microbiome, the collection of microorganisms residing in the gastrointestinal tract, has been found to influence brain function and mental health. Emerging evidence suggests that the gut microbiome can affect neurotransmitter production, inflammation, and stress responses, all of which are crucial for mental health.

For example, studies have shown that probiotics may have a positive impact on mood and anxiety levels, potentially offering new avenues for treatment. Understanding the gut-brain axis provides a holistic perspective on mental health and highlights the importance of lifestyle factors, such as diet and exercise, in promoting psychological well-being.

The stigma surrounding mental health remains a significant barrier to seeking help and treatment. Neuroscience has the potential to challenge misconceptions about mental health disorders by emphasizing their biological basis. By educating the public about the neurobiological underpinnings of mental health conditions, we can promote a more compassionate and informed understanding of these disorders. Increasing awareness and understanding can lead to greater acceptance of mental health issues, encouraging individuals to seek the support and treatment they need.

In addition to addressing stigma, it is essential to consider the cultural context in which mental health is understood and treated. Different cultures have unique perspectives on mental health, which can influence how individuals experience and express their symptoms. Recognizing these cultural differences is crucial for developing culturally sensitive treatment approaches that resonate with diverse populations. Mental health professionals must be aware of the cultural factors that shape individuals' beliefs and attitudes toward mental health, ensuring that interventions are tailored to meet the specific needs of each individual.

The integration of neuroscience into mental health practice also has implications for early intervention and prevention strategies. By understanding the risk factors and biological markers associated with mental health disorders, researchers and clinicians can identify individuals at higher risk and implement preventive measures. Early intervention programs that target at-risk populations can help reduce the incidence of mental health disorders and improve long-term outcomes. This proactive approach emphasizes the importance of mental health promotion and education in schools, workplaces, and communities.

As our understanding of mental health and neuroscience continues to evolve, the importance of interdisciplinary collaboration becomes increasingly evident. Mental health professionals, neuroscientists, educators, and policymakers must work together to develop comprehensive strategies for promoting mental health and well-being. By integrating knowledge from various fields, we can create holistic approaches that address the complex interplay between biology, psychology, and social factors in mental health.

In conclusion, the relationship between mental health and neuroscience is multifaceted, encompassing a range of biological, psychological, and social factors. Advances in neuroscience have deepened our understanding of the brain's role in mental health, shedding light on the neurobiological mechanisms underlying various psychological conditions. By exploring the intricate connections between brain function, neurotransmitters, stress, neuroplasticity, and the gut-brain axis, we can develop more effective interventions and treatment approaches. Additionally, addressing stigma, promoting cultural sensitivity, and fostering interdisciplinary collaboration are essential for advancing mental health care. As we continue to unravel the complexities of mental health and neuroscience, we move closer to a future where individuals can access the support and resources they need to thrive mentally and emotionally.

Nutrition and the Brain

Nutrition plays a pivotal role in brain health and function, influencing not only cognitive performance but also emotional well-being. The brain, despite accounting for only about 2% of total body weight, consumes roughly 20% of the body's energy supply, highlighting its high metabolic demands. This intricate organ requires a wide array of nutrients to maintain optimal function, and deficiencies in essential nutrients can lead to cognitive decline, mood disorders, and various neurological conditions. Understanding the relationship between nutrition and brain health is crucial for fostering optimal cognitive function throughout the lifespan.

The brain is composed of approximately 75% water, making hydration a fundamental aspect of brain health. Even mild dehydration can impair cognitive performance, leading to difficulties in concentration, memory, and mood regulation. Ensuring adequate fluid intake is essential for maintaining optimal brain function. Water aids in the transportation of nutrients to the brain and helps in the removal of waste products. Therefore, maintaining proper hydration levels is vital for overall cognitive health.

Macronutrients—carbohydrates, proteins, and fats—serve as the building blocks for brain health. Carbohydrates are the primary source of energy for the brain, and they are necessary for the synthesis of neurotransmitters, the chemical messengers that facilitate communication between neurons. Complex carbohydrates, such as whole grains, fruits, and vegetables, provide a steady supply of glucose, which is essential for sustained cognitive performance. Conversely, simple carbohydrates found in sugary snacks can lead to rapid spikes and subsequent crashes in blood sugar levels, negatively impacting concentration and mood.

Proteins are essential for the growth and repair of brain cells and are crucial for the production of neurotransmitters. Amino acids, the building blocks of proteins, play a vital role in brain function. For instance, tryptophan is a precursor to serotonin, a neurotransmitter associated with mood regulation. A diet rich in high-quality protein sources, such as lean meats, fish, eggs, legumes, and dairy products, supports optimal neurotransmitter synthesis and overall brain health.

Fats, particularly omega-3 fatty acids, are integral to brain structure and function. The brain is composed of about 60% fat, and omega-3 fatty acids are essential for maintaining the integrity of cell membranes and promoting neuroplasticity—the brain's ability to adapt and reorganize itself. Research has shown that omega-3 fatty acids, found in fatty fish like salmon, walnuts, and flaxseeds, can improve cognitive function and reduce the risk of cognitive decline and dementia. These fatty acids are also anti-inflammatory, helping to protect the brain from oxidative stress and inflammation, both of which can contribute to neurodegenerative diseases.

Vitamins and minerals play crucial roles in maintaining brain health. B vitamins, particularly B6, B12, and folate, are essential for neurotransmitter synthesis and the maintenance of healthy nerve cells. Deficiencies in these vitamins have been linked to cognitive decline and mood disorders. For instance, low levels of vitamin B12 are associated with memory problems and depression. Folate, found in leafy greens, beans, and fortified cereals, is crucial for proper brain development and function. Ensuring adequate intake of B vitamins through a balanced diet can support cognitive health throughout the lifespan.

Antioxidants are compounds that protect the brain from oxidative stress, which can damage cells and contribute to aging and neurodegenerative diseases. Vitamins C and E, as well as flavonoids found in fruits and vegetables, are powerful antioxidants that help neutralize free radicals. A diet rich in colorful fruits and vegetables, such as berries, citrus fruits, and leafy greens, can provide a wide array of antioxidants that support brain health. For example, research has shown that the flavonoids in blueberries may improve memory and cognitive function, highlighting the importance of consuming a variety of antioxidant-rich foods.

The gut-brain axis is an emerging area of research that explores the relationship between gut health and brain function. The gut microbiome, the collection of microorganisms residing in the gastrointestinal tract, plays a significant role in overall health, including brain health. Recent studies have shown that the gut microbiome can influence neurotransmitter production, inflammation, and the body's stress response, all of which are critical for mental well-being. A diet rich in fiber, prebiotics, and probiotics can support a healthy gut microbiome, which in turn may have positive effects on brain health. Foods like yogurt, kefir, sauerkraut, and high-fiber fruits and vegetables can promote the growth of beneficial gut bacteria.

Dietary patterns also play a significant role in brain health. The Mediterranean diet, characterized by high consumption of fruits, vegetables, whole grains, fish, olive oil, and nuts, has been associated with improved cognitive function and a reduced risk of neurodegenerative diseases. Research has shown that adherence to the Mediterranean diet can slow cognitive decline and decrease the risk of Alzheimer's disease. This dietary pattern emphasizes the importance of whole, nutrient-dense foods and healthy fats, which are beneficial for brain health.

In contrast, diets high in processed foods, refined sugars, and unhealthy fats have been linked to negative cognitive outcomes. The standard American diet, which is often high in these unhealthy components, has been associated with an increased risk of obesity, diabetes, and heart disease—all of which are risk factors for cognitive decline and dementia. Reducing the intake of processed foods and sugar-laden snacks can help improve overall health and support cognitive function.

Meal timing and frequency may also influence brain health. Research suggests that regular meal patterns, such as eating every few hours, can help stabilize blood sugar levels and improve cognitive performance. Some studies have shown that intermittent fasting may have neuroprotective effects, promoting brain health and enhancing cognitive function. However, more research is needed to fully understand the implications of meal timing on brain health.

Food can also influence mood and mental well-being. The concept of "food as medicine" emphasizes the idea that certain foods can have therapeutic effects on mental health. For example, omega-3 fatty acids, found in fish, have been shown to reduce symptoms of depression and anxiety. Similarly, complex carbohydrates can enhance the availability of tryptophan, leading to increased serotonin production and improved mood. A balanced diet that includes a variety of nutrient-dense foods can support emotional well-being and cognitive function.

The impact of nutrition on brain health extends beyond dietary choices; it also involves lifestyle factors. Regular physical activity has been shown to enhance brain function and promote neuroplasticity. Exercise increases blood flow to the brain, delivering oxygen and nutrients that support cognitive function. Furthermore, physical activity has been linked to improved mood and reduced symptoms of anxiety and depression. Combining a healthy diet with regular exercise can maximize the benefits for brain health.

Sleep is another critical factor influencing brain health and is closely tied to nutrition. Poor sleep quality can impair cognitive function and emotional regulation, while adequate sleep is essential for memory consolidation and overall brain health. Nutritional choices can affect sleep quality; for instance, foods rich in magnesium, such as nuts and seeds, can promote relaxation and improve sleep quality. Additionally, avoiding caffeine and heavy meals close to bedtime can help support better sleep.

As our understanding of the relationship between nutrition and brain health continues to evolve, it is crucial to prioritize dietary choices that support cognitive function and emotional well-being. Making informed food choices, emphasizing whole foods, and reducing the intake of processed foods can contribute to optimal brain health. Furthermore, adopting a holistic approach that combines nutrition with physical activity, sleep, and stress management can enhance overall well-being and cognitive function.

In conclusion, nutrition is a fundamental aspect of brain health, influencing cognitive performance, emotional well-being, and the risk of neurological disorders. A balanced diet rich in macronutrients, vitamins, minerals, and antioxidants supports optimal brain function and protects against cognitive decline. The gut-brain axis and dietary patterns also play significant roles in overall brain health. By prioritizing nutrient-dense foods and adopting a holistic approach to health, individuals can foster optimal cognitive function and emotional resilience throughout their lives. Emphasizing the importance of nutrition in brain health is essential for promoting overall well-being and preventing mental health disorders.

The Role of Genetics in Brain Function

The intricate relationship between genetics and brain function is a field of study that has garnered significant attention in recent years. Understanding how our genetic makeup influences the development, structure, and function of the brain offers profound insights into the mechanisms underlying various neurological and psychiatric disorders. Genetics plays a crucial role in determining not only our physical traits but also our cognitive abilities, emotional responses, and susceptibility to mental health conditions. This chapter explores the multifaceted role of genetics in brain function, examining how genes interact with environmental factors to shape our neurological landscape.

At the most fundamental level, genes are segments of DNA that contain the instructions for synthesizing proteins, which are the building blocks of the body. The human genome consists of approximately 20,000 to 25,000 genes, each contributing to various biological functions. When it comes to the brain, genes influence its development during prenatal stages, guiding the formation of neural structures and connections. Genetic variations can lead to differences in brain morphology, connectivity, and overall function, ultimately impacting cognitive abilities and behavior.

One of the primary ways in which genetics influences brain function is through the regulation of neurotransmitters—chemical messengers that facilitate communication between neurons. Genes encode for enzymes and proteins involved in the synthesis, release, and uptake of neurotransmitters. For example, variations in genes related to serotonin, dopamine, and norepinephrine can affect mood regulation, reward processing, and overall emotional well-being. Understanding these genetic variations helps elucidate the biological underpinnings of mental health disorders such as depression, anxiety, and schizophrenia.

Furthermore, the role of genetics extends beyond individual neurotransmitter systems. The brain is a highly complex organ characterized by intricate networks of neurons that communicate through synapses. Genetic factors can influence the formation and maintenance of these synaptic connections, shaping how neurons interact and process information. Synaptic plasticity, the ability of synapses to strengthen or weaken over time in response to activity, is essential for learning and memory. Genetic variations that affect synaptic plasticity can thus have profound implications for cognitive function and adaptability.

The field of epigenetics provides additional insights into how genetic factors interact with environmental influences. Epigenetic modifications refer to changes in gene expression that do not involve alterations to the DNA sequence itself. Environmental factors such as diet, stress, and exposure to toxins can lead to epigenetic changes that impact brain function. For instance, studies have shown that stress can trigger epigenetic modifications that alter the expression of genes involved in the stress response, potentially increasing susceptibility to anxiety and depression. This interplay between genetics and the environment underscores the importance of considering both hereditary and lifestyle factors in understanding brain health.

Twin studies have been instrumental in elucidating the genetic contributions to brain function. By comparing the similarities and differences in cognitive abilities and personality traits between identical and fraternal twins, researchers can estimate the heritability of specific traits. For example, studies have shown that genetic factors account for a significant portion of the variance in intelligence, with estimates ranging from 50% to 80%. This indicates that while environmental factors play a role, genetics has a substantial influence on cognitive abilities.

Moreover, advancements in neuroimaging techniques have allowed researchers to explore the genetic basis of brain structure and function in greater detail. For instance, studies using magnetic resonance imaging (MRI) have identified specific genes associated with variations in brain volume, cortical thickness, and connectivity patterns. These findings suggest that certain genetic variants may predispose individuals to structural differences in the brain, which can, in turn, influence cognitive and emotional processes.

The impact of genetics on brain function is further highlighted by the study of neurodevelopmental disorders, such as autism spectrum disorder (ASD) and attention-deficit/hyperactivity disorder (ADHD). Research has identified numerous genetic variants associated with an increased risk of these disorders, suggesting that genetic predisposition plays a critical role in their etiology. For example, copy number variations (CNVs), which involve deletions or duplications of DNA segments, have been linked to an elevated risk of autism. Understanding the genetic underpinnings of these disorders not only aids in diagnosis but also provides avenues for targeted interventions and therapies.

Another significant aspect of genetics in brain function is the study of neurodegenerative diseases, such as Alzheimer's disease and Parkinson's disease. While aging is the primary risk factor for these conditions, genetics also plays a pivotal role. Specific gene variants, such as the APOE ε4 allele, have been associated with an increased risk of developing Alzheimer's disease. Research in this area has led to the identification of potential biomarkers for early detection, enabling more effective management and treatment strategies.

The interplay between genetics and environment is further illustrated by the concept of gene-environment interactions. These interactions occur when specific environmental factors influence the expression of genetic traits. For example, individuals with a genetic predisposition to depression may only develop the disorder when exposed to stressful life events. Understanding these interactions is crucial for developing personalized interventions that consider both genetic and environmental factors.

The field of pharmacogenetics examines how genetic variations influence individual responses to medications, particularly in the context of psychiatric and neurological treatments. Genetic factors can affect drug metabolism, efficacy, and the likelihood of side effects. For instance, variations in the CYP450 gene family, which encodes enzymes involved in drug metabolism, can lead to differences in how individuals process medications such as antidepressants or antipsychotics. Tailoring treatment plans based on an individual's genetic profile can enhance therapeutic outcomes and minimize adverse effects.

Moreover, research in genetics has paved the way for the development of gene therapies and targeted treatments for various neurological and psychiatric disorders. Advances in technologies such as CRISPR-Cas9 have made it possible to edit specific genes associated with diseases, offering potential avenues for curing genetic conditions. While still in its infancy, gene therapy holds promise for addressing disorders with a strong genetic component, such as Huntington's disease and certain forms of muscular dystrophy.

As our understanding of the genetic basis of brain function continues to evolve, ethical considerations surrounding genetic testing and intervention are becoming increasingly important. Issues related to privacy, consent, and the potential for genetic discrimination raise complex ethical questions that must be addressed as we navigate the implications of genetic research. Ensuring that individuals have access to accurate information and support is essential for making informed decisions regarding genetic testing and potential interventions.

In summary, genetics plays a critical role in shaping brain function, influencing everything from neurotransmitter systems and synaptic plasticity to cognitive abilities and emotional responses. The interplay between genetic and environmental factors underscores the complexity of brain health and the importance of a holistic approach to understanding neurological and psychiatric disorders. Advances in genetics and neuroimaging techniques continue to shed light on the mechanisms underlying brain function, paving the way for targeted interventions and personalized treatments. As we delve deeper into the genetic basis of brain health, it is imperative to consider the ethical implications and ensure that individuals have access to the information and resources they need to make informed choices about their health.

Brain Development Across the Lifespan

Brain development is a complex and dynamic process that occurs throughout an individual's lifespan. From the moment of conception to late adulthood, the brain undergoes significant changes in structure and function that are influenced by a variety of genetic, environmental, and experiential factors. Understanding how the brain develops across different life stages is crucial for grasping the foundations of cognitive and emotional processes, as well as the impact of various interventions and experiences on brain health.

The journey of brain development begins during prenatal stages. The human brain starts to form shortly after conception, with the neural tube developing around the third week of gestation. This tube eventually gives rise to the entire central nervous system, including the brain and spinal cord. As development progresses, neural progenitor cells proliferate, differentiate, and migrate to their designated locations, forming the different regions of the brain. By the end of the first trimester, the basic structures of the brain are established, and the foundation for future growth is laid.

During this early period, the environment plays a critical role in brain development. Factors such as maternal nutrition, exposure to toxins, and stress can significantly influence the formation of neural connections and the overall health of the developing brain. For instance, maternal malnutrition during pregnancy has been linked to deficits in cognitive function and emotional regulation in offspring. Additionally, exposure to teratogens, such as alcohol and certain drugs, can result in developmental disorders, highlighting the importance of a healthy prenatal environment.

As the child enters infancy and early childhood, the brain continues to undergo rapid growth and maturation. At birth, the brain is approximately 25% of its adult size, but by the age of two, it reaches about 80% of its adult size. This period is characterized by a remarkable increase in the number of synapses, the connections between neurons that facilitate communication. During the first few years of life, the brain experiences a phenomenon known as synaptogenesis, in which the formation of new synapses occurs at an extraordinary rate. This process is influenced by both genetic programming and environmental stimulation, as experiences shape the development of neural pathways.

Critical periods of development emerge during this stage, where certain experiences are essential for optimal brain maturation. For example, the development of vision and language relies on exposure to visual and auditory stimuli during specific windows of time. Children who are deprived of these experiences during critical periods may face difficulties in acquiring necessary skills later in life. This emphasizes the importance of early interventions and enriching environments to support healthy brain development.

The concept of plasticity is central to understanding brain development during childhood. Neural plasticity refers to the brain's ability to reorganize and adapt in response to experiences. This capacity for change is particularly pronounced during childhood when the brain is more receptive to learning and acquiring new skills. Engaging in stimulating activities, such as play, social interactions, and education, can enhance neural connections and foster cognitive development.

As children transition into adolescence, the brain undergoes further transformations that are influenced by hormonal changes and the maturation of brain regions.

Adolescence is marked by the development of the prefrontal cortex, which is responsible for higher-order cognitive functions such as decision-making, impulse control, and reasoning. While the prefrontal cortex is still maturing during this stage, the limbic system, which governs emotions and reward processing, is fully developed. This imbalance can contribute to risk-taking behavior and emotional fluctuations commonly observed during adolescence.

The adolescent brain is particularly sensitive to social and emotional experiences. Peer relationships and social interactions play a crucial role in shaping identity and behavior during this stage. The developing brain is wired to seek social connections, which can lead to both positive and negative outcomes. Understanding the neurobiological underpinnings of adolescent behavior can inform approaches to support healthy decision-making and emotional regulation during this critical period.

Entering adulthood, the brain reaches its peak in terms of structure and function. While the physical growth of the brain slows down, maturation continues, particularly in the prefrontal cortex. This region is essential for executive functions, which include planning, problem-solving, and self-regulation. Adult brain development is characterized by a process known as myelination, where nerve fibers are insulated with a fatty substance called myelin. This enhances the efficiency of neural communication, facilitating quicker processing and transmission of information.

Throughout adulthood, the brain remains capable of change and adaptation, although the rate of neuroplasticity decreases compared to childhood. Experiences, learning, and lifestyle choices continue to shape the brain's structure and function. Engaging in mentally stimulating activities, physical exercise, and social interactions can promote cognitive health and resilience against age-related decline. Moreover, the brain's ability to form new neurons, a process known as neurogenesis, continues into adulthood, particularly in regions such as the hippocampus, which is involved in learning and memory.

As individuals age, the brain undergoes natural changes that can impact cognitive function. Age-related decline in certain cognitive abilities, such as processing speed and working memory, is common. However, it is essential to recognize that not all cognitive functions decline with age; many individuals maintain strong verbal skills, knowledge, and wisdom well into their later years. Factors such as genetics, lifestyle, and overall health significantly influence cognitive aging and brain resilience.

Research has shown that engaging in activities that challenge the brain, such as learning new skills or hobbies, can help mitigate cognitive decline. Furthermore, maintaining a healthy lifestyle that includes regular physical exercise, a balanced diet, and social engagement contributes to brain health. Studies have indicated that lifestyle factors can influence the expression of genes associated with cognitive function and neurodegenerative diseases, emphasizing the importance of proactive measures for maintaining brain health throughout the lifespan.

Neurodegenerative diseases, such as Alzheimer's disease and Parkinson's disease, become more prevalent as individuals age. These conditions are characterized by progressive cognitive decline and motor impairment. Understanding the underlying mechanisms of these diseases is crucial for developing effective interventions and treatments. Genetic factors, environmental influences, and lifestyle choices all play a role in the risk of developing neurodegenerative disorders.

In recent years, advancements in neuroimaging techniques have provided valuable insights into the aging brain. Functional magnetic resonance imaging (fMRI) and positron emission tomography (PET) scans allow researchers to observe brain activity and metabolic processes in real time. These tools have contributed to a better understanding of the neural correlates of cognitive aging, providing a clearer picture of how brain function changes over time.

While brain development is often viewed as a linear process, it is important to recognize that individuals may experience unique trajectories based on a variety of factors, including genetics, environment, and life experiences. The concept of resilience highlights the brain's capacity to adapt and recover from challenges, whether they be psychological stressors, injuries, or neurodegenerative diseases. Understanding the factors that contribute to resilience can inform strategies for promoting mental health and well-being across the lifespan.

In summary, brain development is a lifelong journey characterized by continuous growth, adaptation, and change. From prenatal stages through late adulthood, the brain is shaped by a complex interplay of genetic, environmental, and experiential factors. Understanding the stages of brain development and the influences that shape cognitive and emotional processes is essential for promoting healthy brain function and resilience throughout life. As research in neuroscience continues to evolve, it holds the promise of informing interventions and strategies to enhance brain health, ultimately supporting individuals in navigating the challenges and opportunities presented at every stage of life.

Learning and Intelligence

Learning and intelligence are two interconnected concepts that shape human behavior, influence personal development, and drive cultural evolution. The intricacies of how we learn and the varying expressions of intelligence form a complex landscape that researchers, educators, and psychologists seek to understand. This exploration spans the definitions, theories, and applications of learning and intelligence, highlighting their significance in our daily lives and the broader context of society.

Learning is often defined as a relatively permanent change in behavior or knowledge that results from experience. It is a fundamental aspect of human existence, allowing individuals to adapt to their environments, acquire new skills, and refine their understanding of the world. Learning can occur in various forms, including classical conditioning, operant conditioning, observational learning, and cognitive learning. Each type provides a framework for understanding how behaviors and knowledge are acquired and modified over time.

Classical conditioning, first described by Ivan Pavlov, involves learning through association. In his famous experiment with dogs, Pavlov demonstrated that a neutral stimulus, when paired repeatedly with an unconditioned stimulus, could elicit a conditioned response. This principle of associative learning has far-reaching implications in various domains, from behavioral therapies to marketing strategies. It illustrates how individuals can learn to associate certain stimuli with specific outcomes, shaping their responses in predictable ways.

Operant conditioning, developed by B.F. Skinner, emphasizes the role of reinforcement and punishment in learning. According to this theory, behaviors are influenced by their consequences; behaviors that are rewarded are likely to be repeated, while those that are punished are less likely to occur. This concept is fundamental in educational settings and behavior modification programs, where positive reinforcement is often used to encourage desired behaviors. The principles of operant conditioning are also applicable in everyday life, such as when parents reward their children for good behavior or when individuals strive to achieve personal goals through self-reward systems.

Observational learning, proposed by Albert Bandura, posits that individuals can learn by observing the behaviors of others. Bandura's famous Bobo doll experiment demonstrated that children who observed aggressive behavior toward a doll were more likely to imitate that behavior themselves. This highlights the importance of social models in shaping learning and behavior, as individuals often look to others for cues on how to act in various situations. Observational learning plays a crucial role in cultural transmission, where norms, values, and skills are passed down through generations.

Cognitive learning theory focuses on the mental processes involved in learning. It emphasizes the role of internal cognitive structures and processes, such as attention, memory, and problem-solving. Cognitive learning theorists argue that learning is not merely a response to stimuli but involves active processing of information. Techniques such as mnemonic devices, concept mapping, and self-regulated learning strategies reflect the cognitive approach to education, promoting deeper understanding and retention of knowledge.

Intelligence, on the other hand, is a multifaceted construct that encompasses a range of cognitive abilities, including reasoning, problem-solving, comprehension, and adaptability. The definition of intelligence has evolved over time, with various theories emerging to explain its nature and manifestations. Early theories, such as Charles

Spearman's g factor, posited a single general intelligence that underlies all cognitive abilities. In contrast, Howard Gardner's theory of multiple intelligences expanded the definition of intelligence to include diverse modalities, such as linguistic, logical-mathematical, spatial, musical, bodily-kinesthetic, interpersonal, intrapersonal, and naturalistic intelligences.

Gardner's theory challenges the traditional notion of intelligence as solely measured by IQ tests, which often focus on linguistic and logical reasoning skills. By recognizing multiple intelligences, Gardner encourages educators to adopt a more holistic approach to learning, tailoring instruction to accommodate diverse talents and learning styles. This perspective emphasizes the importance of fostering individual strengths and interests, promoting engagement and motivation in the learning process.

Emotional intelligence, popularized by Daniel Goleman, represents another significant dimension of intelligence. It refers to the ability to recognize, understand, and manage one's own emotions while also recognizing and influencing the emotions of others. Emotional intelligence plays a vital role in interpersonal relationships, communication, and leadership. Individuals with high emotional intelligence are often better equipped to navigate social situations, resolve conflicts, and foster collaboration, underscoring the importance of emotional awareness in both personal and professional contexts.

The relationship between learning and intelligence is reciprocal. Intelligence influences the capacity for learning, while learning experiences can enhance cognitive abilities. Individuals with higher intelligence may have an easier time grasping complex concepts, processing information efficiently, and applying knowledge to novel situations. Conversely, engaging in diverse learning experiences can lead to the development of critical thinking skills, creativity, and adaptability, contributing to a more nuanced understanding of intelligence.

Moreover, the role of motivation in learning and intelligence cannot be overstated. Motivation drives individuals to pursue knowledge, tackle challenges, and persist in the face of difficulties. Intrinsic motivation, which arises from a genuine interest in the subject matter, often leads to deeper engagement and mastery of skills. In contrast, extrinsic motivation, driven by external rewards or pressures, may yield superficial learning outcomes. Understanding the motivational factors that influence learning can inform educational practices and enhance the overall effectiveness of teaching strategies.

In recent years, advancements in neuroscience have provided valuable insights into the biological underpinnings of learning and intelligence. Neuroplasticity, the brain's ability to reorganize itself in response to experience, underscores the dynamic nature of learning. Research has shown that engaging in challenging cognitive tasks can lead to structural changes in the brain, enhancing neural connections and promoting cognitive flexibility. This knowledge highlights the potential for lifelong learning and the importance of maintaining cognitive engagement throughout the lifespan.

Furthermore, the influence of environmental factors on learning and intelligence is significant. Socioeconomic status, access to education, cultural values, and family support all play crucial roles in shaping cognitive development and learning outcomes. Disparities in educational opportunities can lead to differences in intelligence test scores and academic achievement, emphasizing the need for equitable access to quality education for all individuals. Addressing these disparities is essential for fostering a society that values and nurtures the potential of every learner.

Cultural factors also impact perceptions of intelligence and learning. Different cultures may prioritize varying skills and knowledge, shaping the ways in which intelligence is defined and evaluated. For instance, collectivist cultures may emphasize social harmony and interpersonal relationships, valuing emotional intelligence and collaboration over individual achievement. In contrast, individualistic cultures may prioritize analytical reasoning and competition. Understanding these cultural dimensions is essential for creating inclusive educational environments that respect and celebrate diverse ways of knowing and learning.

Incorporating technology into learning has transformed the educational landscape. Digital tools and online platforms offer innovative ways to facilitate learning and intelligence development. E-learning, interactive simulations, and educational apps can provide personalized learning experiences that cater to individual needs and preferences. However, it is essential to balance technology use with traditional methods to ensure a comprehensive and well-rounded educational experience. Educators must also be mindful of the potential pitfalls of technology, such as distractions and information overload, which can hinder the learning process.

As we delve into the future of learning and intelligence, it is crucial to consider the implications of artificial intelligence (AI) and machine learning. AI systems have the potential to revolutionize education by providing personalized learning experiences, analyzing data to inform instructional strategies, and even facilitating adaptive learning environments. However, ethical considerations must guide the integration of AI in education, ensuring that technology enhances rather than detracts from the human aspects of learning.

In conclusion, learning and intelligence are multifaceted constructs that shape individual growth and societal progress. Understanding the various dimensions of learning, the diverse expressions of intelligence, and the interplay between these concepts is essential for fostering effective educational practices and promoting lifelong learning. As we navigate the complexities of learning and intelligence, it is crucial to recognize the unique strengths of each individual and to create inclusive environments that nurture potential, encourage exploration, and celebrate the diversity of human experience. By doing so, we can empower individuals to thrive in an ever-changing world and contribute meaningfully to their communities and society at large.

The Future of Neuroscience

As we venture further into the 21st century, the field of neuroscience stands at the precipice of unprecedented growth and innovation. The integration of advanced technologies, interdisciplinary collaboration, and an increasing understanding of the complexities of the brain heralds a new era in the study of neural processes. The future of neuroscience promises not only to deepen our understanding of the brain's intricate workings but also to translate this knowledge into tangible applications that enhance human health, cognition, and overall well-being.

One of the most exciting frontiers in neuroscience is the advent of neurotechnology. This rapidly evolving field encompasses a wide range of tools and techniques designed to interface with the nervous system. Brain-computer interfaces (BCIs), for example, allow for direct communication between the brain and external devices. These systems have the potential to revolutionize how we interact with technology, enabling individuals with mobility impairments to control prosthetic limbs, communicate via computer interfaces, or even manipulate their environment through thought alone. As BCIs become more refined and accessible, they could transform the lives of millions, restoring autonomy and improving quality of life.

Moreover, the integration of artificial intelligence (AI) and machine learning in neuroscience is poised to accelerate research and clinical applications. AI algorithms can analyze vast amounts of data, identifying patterns and correlations that may be imperceptible to human researchers. For instance, deep learning techniques have been employed to improve the accuracy of brain imaging analysis, allowing for more precise diagnoses of neurological disorders. The synergy between AI and neuroscience has the potential to enhance our understanding of brain function, optimize treatment plans, and personalize interventions for individuals suffering from conditions such as epilepsy, depression, and Alzheimer's disease.

In addition to technological advancements, the future of neuroscience is being shaped by a growing recognition of the brain's plasticity and adaptability. Neuroplasticity, the brain's ability to reorganize itself in response to experience, is a fundamental principle that underlies learning, recovery from injury, and the development of new skills. As we gain a deeper understanding of the mechanisms driving neuroplasticity, researchers are exploring novel therapeutic approaches to harness this capacity for change. For example, rehabilitation programs that incorporate targeted cognitive training and physical activity are showing promise in facilitating recovery from stroke and traumatic brain injury, underscoring the brain's remarkable ability to heal and adapt.

Another critical area of exploration in the future of neuroscience is the interplay between genetics and environment in shaping brain function and behavior. The field of neurogenetics is burgeoning, as researchers investigate how genetic variations influence neural development, cognition, and susceptibility to mental health disorders. The mapping of the human genome has provided valuable insights into the genetic basis of various conditions, from schizophrenia to autism spectrum disorder. Understanding the genetic underpinnings of these disorders can inform targeted interventions, paving the way for precision medicine approaches that consider an individual's unique genetic profile.

Furthermore, the impact of environmental factors on brain development and function is increasingly recognized. Factors such as stress, nutrition, and early-life experiences can significantly influence neural architecture and cognitive outcomes. The emerging field of epigenetics explores how environmental influences can affect gene expression without altering the underlying DNA sequence. This knowledge has profound implications for public health and education, emphasizing the importance of creating supportive environments that foster optimal brain development from an early age.

The future of neuroscience also promises to deepen our understanding of the relationship between brain health and overall well-being. Mental health has garnered significant attention in recent years, with increasing recognition of the prevalence and impact of mental health disorders worldwide. Neuroscience is playing a crucial role in unraveling the complex biological, psychological, and social factors that contribute to mental health. Advances in neuroimaging and biomarker identification are paving the way for more accurate diagnoses and effective treatments for conditions such as anxiety, depression, and bipolar disorder.

Moreover, the stigma surrounding mental health is gradually diminishing, fostering a more open dialogue about psychological well-being. Public awareness campaigns, increased funding for mental health research, and advocacy efforts are driving progress in the field. As neuroscience continues to elucidate the biological mechanisms underlying mental health disorders, it is imperative that we translate this knowledge into accessible interventions and support systems that prioritize mental well-being.

In parallel with advancements in mental health research, the future of neuroscience is being shaped by a growing focus on brain health across the lifespan. Understanding how the brain ages and how age-related cognitive decline can be mitigated is a pressing concern in our increasingly aging population. Research is exploring the impact of lifestyle factors such as diet, exercise, and social engagement on brain health, with promising findings suggesting that certain interventions may promote cognitive resilience and slow the onset of neurodegenerative diseases.

Additionally, the development of innovative neuroprotective strategies is on the rise. Researchers are investigating pharmacological and non-pharmacological interventions that may safeguard the brain from age-related decline. Nutraceuticals, exercise, cognitive training, and social engagement are all areas of exploration that may hold the key to promoting healthy aging and preventing cognitive impairment.

As we look ahead, the ethical implications of advancements in neuroscience cannot be overlooked. The ability to manipulate neural activity and understand the neural correlates of consciousness raises important questions about privacy, consent, and the potential for misuse of neurotechnology. Ethical considerations must guide the development and application of these technologies, ensuring that they are used responsibly and with respect for individual autonomy.

Moreover, the intersection of neuroscience with fields such as philosophy, law, and sociology presents opportunities for interdisciplinary collaboration. Understanding the implications of neuroscience for concepts such as free will, personal responsibility, and criminal behavior requires nuanced discussions that integrate insights from multiple disciplines. As neuroscience continues to evolve, fostering dialogue across fields will be essential to navigate the complex ethical terrain it presents.

The globalization of neuroscience research is also a noteworthy trend. Collaborative efforts across countries and cultures are fostering a more inclusive and diverse scientific community. International partnerships enable researchers to share knowledge, resources, and expertise, driving innovation and accelerating progress. As we face global challenges such as mental health crises and neurological disorders, collaborative research initiatives hold the potential to address these issues on a broader scale.

Furthermore, the integration of neuroscience education into curricula at all levels is vital for fostering a future generation of informed citizens and researchers. By increasing awareness of brain health and the principles of neuroscience, we can empower individuals to make informed decisions about their well-being. Early education initiatives that promote an understanding of the brain and its functions can also lay the foundation for future research and innovation in the field.

The future of neuroscience is characterized by a commitment to promoting brain health, enhancing cognitive functioning, and addressing the challenges posed by neurological and mental health disorders. As we continue to uncover the complexities of the brain, the implications for society are profound. The knowledge gained from neuroscience research has the potential to inform public policy, healthcare practices, and educational strategies, ultimately improving the lives of individuals and communities.

In conclusion, the future of neuroscience holds tremendous promise. With advancements in technology, interdisciplinary collaboration, and a deepening understanding of the brain's complexities, we are poised to make significant strides in understanding brain function, enhancing mental health, and promoting cognitive resilience. By addressing the ethical implications, fostering global collaboration, and prioritizing education, we can harness the power of neuroscience to create a healthier and more informed society. The journey ahead is filled with opportunities for discovery, innovation, and positive change, paving the way for a future where the mysteries of the brain are unraveled, and the potential of human cognition is fully realized.

Acknowledgments

I would like to express my heartfelt gratitude to my family for their unwavering support and encouragement throughout this journey. Their belief in me has been a constant source of motivation, inspiring me to delve deep into the complexities of the brain and share my findings with the world.

To my readers, thank you for taking the time to explore this work. Your interest in understanding how the brain functions is what drives the passion behind this project. I hope the insights presented here resonate with you and enrich your understanding of the fascinating world of neuroscience.

If you have enjoyed this exploration into the workings of the brain, I invite you to leave a review on Amazon. Your feedback not only helps me improve my future works but also assists fellow readers in discovering the value of this content. Thank you for your support!